Greenhill

# The Sky
# My Kingdom

**GREENHILL
MILITARY PAPERBACKS**

# The Sky My Kingdom

## HANNA REITSCH

Greenhill Books, London
Stackpole Books, Pennsylvania

Greenhill Books

This edition of *The Sky My Kingdom*
first published 1997 by
Greenhill Books, Lionel Leventhal Limited
Park House, 1 Russell Gardens, London NW11 9NN
and
Stackpole Books, 5067 Ritter Road, Mechanicsburg, PA 17055, USA

*British Library Cataloguing in Publication Data available*

ISBN 1-85367-262-9

*Library of Congress Cataloging-in-Publication Data available*

Publishing History
*The Sky My Kingdom* was first published in English in 1955
(The Bodley Head), was reprinted in 1991 by Greenhill Books,
with the addition of some additional photographs and a Postscript,
and is reproduced now in paperback, complete and unabridged.

Printed and bound in Great Britain by
Biddles Limited, Guildford and King's Lynn.

# Contents

# List of Illustrations

## 1.  The Child that Watched the Sky

WHAT CHILD is there that lives, as I did, midway between Reality and Fairyland, that does not long sometimes to leave altogether the familiar world and set off in search of new and fabulous realms?

Such dreams have always visited Mankind, are born, first, in the open and eager minds of children and find in flying their fulfilment. My parents had shown me as a child the storks in their quiet and steady flight, the buzzards, circling ever higher in the summer air and so, when I, too, expressed a longing to fly, they took it for a childish fancy, that like so many of our youthful enthusiasms, would be forgotten with the years.

But the longing grew in me, grew with every bird I saw go flying across the azure summer sky, with every cloud that sailed past me on the wind, till it turned to a deep, insistent homesickness, a yearning that went with me everywhere and could never be stilled.

My father was an eye-specialist and head of a private eye-clinic in Hirschberg, Silesia, where we lived. From an early age, I took it in turns with my brother, Kurt, to accompany him on his daily rounds in the clinic, regaling the patients with childish gifts which I had made myself and later, when I visited them on my way home from school, with stories of my adventures, both real and imaginary.

My father was a born doctor and though I was too young to realise it then, I noticed and was impressed by the personal care and attention which he lavished on each of his patients. Later I came to know that helping and healing had so come to fill his life that his work as a doctor gave him complete happiness. Any sphere of activity, for example a University appointment, that would have deprived him of his patients he never seriously considered and offers in this direction were invariably rejected. Perhaps for that reason, he was particularly pleased to see me take an early, still quite childish, interest in his medical activities.

Thus I soon acquired an interest in my father's work and, for his part, he spared no pains to encourage me, obtaining, for example, from the butcher the eyes of dead animals to show me their construction and how small operations could be performed.

My mother had been brought up as a Catholic and although we followed my father's denomination and lived as Protestants, her Catholic background retained its influence. This situation caused her some difficulties of conscience, but not wishing to upset my father, she kept them to herself and I only heard of them much later. I often used to kneel beside her when she interrupted her daily affairs to pay a short visit to church and though she did not know it, it was by her personal example that she gave her children the most convincing lessons in piety.

Once my mother had had forebodings that she would die at my birth, but when the time came—it was a stormy night in Spring—they proved unfounded, for she recovered normally and was able, some years later, to have another child.

For that reason, perhaps, despite her unbounded love for my brother and sister, she felt particularly close to me, as I did to her, though I, too, loved each member of my family equally. My mother and I lived in each other, each sensing the other's thoughts without need to confess or conceal, and to us, it was as natural as any other of Nature's mysteries, which remain no less mysterious for being evident to all.

In our family, it was accepted as a principle, so obvious as to be unspoken, that a girl could only have one task in life, namely, to marry and become a good mother to her children. Owing to my interest in medicine, however, also to my mother's religious example and the recent experience of my own confirmation, I decided, when I was about thirteen or fourteen, that I wanted to become a doctor—not an ordinary one, but a missionary doctor, and not only that, but also, and above all, a flying missionary doctor.

When my father saw the persistence with which I stressed this aspect of my future career, he took me on one side and suggested I make a pact with him. If I could succeed in not mentioning another word about flying until, in two or three years' time, I had passed my school leaving certificate, then he would allow me, as a reward, to partake in a training course in gliding at Grunau, which was not far from Hirschberg and where there was a well-known School for Glider Pilots. By extracting this promise, my father hoped to make me forget the subject of flying, once and for all.

But though, from now on, I was careful not to allow them to cross my lips, my thoughts and dreams of flying continued and my father little knew how often I pedalled out secretly to Grunau, to gaze enviously from the road at the slides, hops and flights of the glider pupils on the Galgenberg.

In maintaining my self-imposed silence, a fortunate chance came to my aid. I came across a book of spiritual exercises by Ignatius of Loyola, "Meditations," I think they were called, which, young as I was, made a great impression on me. They set out to teach the attainment of self-mastery and the eradication of spiritual faults by means of repeated self-examination.

These exercises I undertook with energetic zeal, determining, first, to cure my excessive use of superlatives. It cost me an enormous effort, but, after a while and in spite of many relapses, I was able to record a small improvement, which my mother, who knew nothing of these exercises, to my great joy finally noticed and commented upon.

That small book helped me also to keep silent where I had longed to speak and for a whole two years and more I never once mentioned at home the subject of flying. When I passed my final school examination, my father wanted to present me with an antique gold watch. I quietly returned it to him, reminding him of his promise. I saw him turn pale as he agreed to fulfil it—then my mother clasped me in her arms.

Before I started my medical studies, my parents wished me to attend a School of Domestic Science. I went to the

Colonial School for Women at Rendsburg, which had an excellent reputation and could assist me in preparing for my career of medical missionary. Besides cooking and laundry work, we were taught there how to look after chickens, ducks, geese, pigs and other animals. Cobbling, glazing and locksmithing were compulsory subjects and we could learn to ride and shoot in our spare time. As the curriculum had been designed to prepare women for life in the colonies, we had also to study English and Spanish and either the language of the Kisuaheli Tribe or of the Herreros of South-West Africa.

Rendsburg is in the Province of Holstein and the school lay on the outskirts of the town, alongside the Kiel Canal. The Navy, therefore, was to us pupils a constant source of joy. Every warship that came through the Canal knew the girls' school and whenever we heard a warning siren in the distance, we would rush pell-mell from kitchen, laundry, garden and stables to draw ourselves up in line along the bank of the Canal. As it approached, the warship would slacken speed and then go gliding solemnly past us, while from ship to bank and back again would ring out our shouts of vociferous greeting.

Our schooling lasted a year and the only notable success I was able to record during the whole of my time there was in an experiment which I conducted with the pigs.

At least twice while we were at the school, each of us had to look after the pigs for a week. It was quite a popular duty so long as they were small and manageable, but as they grew older, they lost their attractive qualities and became really treacherous and savage. The task of tending them then became a hateful one. Perhaps the pigs were disturbed by the repeated change in their keeper, but, whatever the reason for their bad temper, every pupil who performed that office after they had grown to full size had the most terrifying tales to tell of her charges' efforts to bite her, until finally it was decided they must be slaughtered. A week before that was due to occur, the duty of pig-keeper fell to me.

The night before my first meeting with my charges I slept

little and at four o'clock the following morning—an hour
before the appointed time—I was already making the first,
tentative approaches so that, in the event of mishaps, I
should avoid the ridicule of the Superintendent Pig-Keeper
who came at five o'clock.

And so, in wooden clogs and rubber apron and armed
with a pitchfork, I set to work in the pig-sty. As ill luck would
have it, on this particular morning, the inmates were more
than usually disgruntled at being disturbed in their slumbers
and fell upon me with concerted venom. Two of them set
about my apron, rending it into tiny shreds, while a third
hurled itself at the pitchfork with which I was attempting to
ward off his fellow-conspirators. With unbelievable strength,
it bit the pole in two and then I fled in panic, still clinging to
the upper end and slamming the door of the sty behind me.

My life I had saved—but what now? The sty had to be
cleaned, though at the mere thought of it, I began to per-
spire with terror. Then I discovered that, built on to the first
sty, was a second one, unused. The two were connected by
an opening covered with a drop-hatch. I cleared the
gardening tools out of the second sty, drove the pigs through
with a broom handle, then let the hatch down and cleaned
out the first sty undisturbed.

The solution seemed ideal, but it had one disadvantage—
I now had two pig-sties to keep clean instead of one! As a
remedy, I decided to train the animals to use the first sty,
now clean and furnished with fresh straw, as their dining-
cum-sitting room and to use the second as a convenience.
This distinction it took the pigs some time to appreciate and
meanwhile I was kept constantly busy, removing their
blemishes from the straw of the day-room to transfer them to
the place where they belonged, first holding the pitchfork
before the nose of the offending animal and administering a
gentle slap.

My fellow pupils watched these efforts with unconcealed
derision and, indeed, for the first three days, the results were
entirely negative. But the fourth day brought a remarkable
change—the day-room was spotless! And so it remained

until, in accordance with Fate's irrevocable decree, the inmates were called upon to surrender their lives.

So, with this modest triumph, my schooldays came to an end.

## 2. I Take to the Air

A ND NOW I was to be allowed to take part in a training course at the School of Gliding in Grunau.

I was to fly at last!

The longed-for day arrived, clear and cloudless. I took my bicycle and riding through Hirschberg made towards the Galgenberg, the familiar houses gradually thinning out into open meadows and fields, while the ridge of the Silesian mountains seemed to smile down at me in the cool, morning air. It was still early and as my feet trod the pedals, the sky above was gleaming a tender blue, the birds were singing and my heart was filled with joy.

On the crest of the Galgenberg was little to attract the eye of the layman, a large hangar where the gliders were kept and, beside it, a small wooden building which served as canteen and provided shelter in bad weather. But the sight made my heart beat higher—here began a new and fascinating world! Full of confidence and hope, shivering with excitement, I stood in a group of young men round the glider, which had already been brought out into the open, and listened as Pit van Husen, the instructor in charge of the course, began his first lesson.

In gliding, you do not begin with theory. Practice and experience mean everything.

First, every glider-pilot must learn to balance.

After others had practiced this, it was my turn.

With thumping heart, I sat down on the open seat of the "Grunau 9." I was five feet-and-half-an-inch tall and

weighed just under 6 stone 6,—and I was a girl! No wonder
the young men standing round made some rude remarks, for
any sensible girl stays in the kitchen!

Pit van Husen held one wing-tip of the glider. Nevertheless it quivered at the slightest movement like a frightened
bird, ready at any moment to tip over on to the ground.
Then he let go the wing-tip and I tried balancing the plane
with the ailerons, as I had been told, keeping the wings level.

After me, others had a try. Some were good, some were
not, hardly any were praised but for anyone who botched it,
there was plenty of comment and not a few were blushing to
the roots of their hair as they stepped out of the plane. But
before we had finished, everyone had managed to balance
the plane.

Next, we practiced ground slides. On Pit van Husen's
orders, some strong lads first fixed the two-legged rubber
cable, or "bunje," into the hook in the nose. Four men were
now stationed at each end of the cable, holding it firm while
others held on to the tail of the glider.

Pit van Husen now gave the orders:

"Heave!"

The men on the cable had to walk forward, heaving on the
ends.

"Double!" And the team ran forward, stretching out the
cable as far as it would go.

"Away!" The tail was let go and the glider was catapulted
forward, sliding over the ground, while the ring of the bunje
dropped away from the vertical post in the nose. During the
short slide, the pilot had then to take care to keep the wings
level and by pressing on the foot pedals which controlled the
rudder, maintain his direction.

Later, we were told, the bunje would be drawn tighter so
that from the slide we would go into short hops of only a few
yards just above the ground. These would gradually become
longer and higher until we started to do short gliding flights,
which could be extended by starting each time from a point
higher up the slope of the hill. The "A" Test required a
flying time of thirty seconds.

Flying does not seem difficult, I thought, as at last my turn
came for a ground slide and I climbed into the plane. How
would it be if I pulled back the stick just a fraction, without
anyone noticing? Would the "crate" take me a yard or so up
into the air? I wanted to start flying, at last.

But the team thought: "We'll give her a real start, this
time" and, on the order "Double," they charged forward
with a roar, stretching the bunje for all it was worth.

Well, let them!...

"Away!" yelled the instructor and in the same instant, I
knew I was going to carry out my threat. I would pull back
the stick a little, not far, at the most six or seven inches,
although it was forbidden!

I did so.

At first, for a second or two, I did not know what was
happening. I felt only how the plane, with myself strapped
inside it, jerked suddenly forward, throwing my head back.
Then, when I came to, I realised that I was no longer sliding,
as I was actually supposed to be, on the ground, but was
flying, and I could see nothing but sky, and then, sky again.
With my feather weight, the team's far too powerful a start
and my pull on the stick, the plane had shot steeply, almost
vertically upward.

"Down!" I heard somebody roar from below, "down!"
And I pushed the stick right down as far as it would go. The
plane had enough speed to follow the stick and the nose
plunged almost vertically towards the earth. Strange, indeed!
I pulled the stick up again,—again, we climbed, again I saw
nothing but sky,—then earth,—then sky. Then,—I noticed
the air-speed had dropped right down—there was a crash,
ripping the straps,—and I lay below. I had been thrown out.
But the glider was intact. I had imagined flying to be somewhat tamer; this up-and-down business was plentifully
exciting.

The boys came charging down in a yelling mob. Of course
she'd make a mess of it, the girl should have stayed in the
kitchen, where she belonged! While their jibes continued, I
got to my feet, laughing as if nothing had happened. But I

had forgotten the instructor. Out of breath from running so fast, Pit van Husen now stood before me, to bellow out such a torrent of words that I was left numbed and deafened. But so much I did understand: I had been disobedient, undisciplined and was completely unfitted for flying.

Then came the shattering blow:

"As a punishment," he yelled, "you will be grounded for three days!"

Thereupon he turned on his heel and left me. With him went some of the pupils, their ardour considerably dampened, while others helped me to load up the plane and haul it back to the launching site. For the rest of that course, I was known to everyone as the "Stratosphere."

As I rode home that evening in utter dejection, I told myself that, though I had been undisciplined and disobedient, I was not "completely unfitted for flying." On this point, Pit van Husen was wrong—and I would prove it.

Fortunately, I was not to know that almost at that very moment the decision was being reached to drop me at the earliest opportunity from the course. That evening, as always at the close of training, Pit van Husen reported on the day's events to Wolf Hirth, the patriarch of gliding and Head of the Grunau Training School. My incident was naturally in the forefront of conversation.

"We must get rid of the girl," Wolf Hirth said calmly, when he had heard the story, "we don't want any corpses."

Of this I knew nothing, either then or in the days that followed. On reaching home, I evaded my family's questions with the plea of being overtired and, locking myself in my room, went straight to bed. But there could be no question of sleep—my thoughts went grinding on like a mill-wheel. Of course, Pit van Husen had been right, a thousand times over! In flying, disobedience of a definite instruction was as bad, almost, as a capital offence. Even the smallest underestimation of the danger involved could have terrible consequences, of which one's own death need not necessarily be the worst. I told myself again and again, till the thought burnt in on my mind, that in gliding the strictest adherence to rules and regulations, even the smallest, was the one un-breakable law. It is thanks perhaps in part to this principle which I adopted for myself that I am still alive today.

The night seemed never to end and the longer I thought, the more doubt grew in my mind. Might it not be that Pit van Husen had been right after all and that I was, indeed, completely unfitted for flying? The thought would not let me rest. I had to do something. Suddenly, I had an idea.

I got up and looked round the room for a walking stick. Then I jumped back into bed and sat there, with the stick between my knees, in the same position as in the pilot's seat of the glider. I closed my eyes and pictured myself sitting in the plane. Then I began to balance, making the same movements with the stick as one did with the control column to prevent either wing-tip from touching the ground.

Then I gave myself the orders to start, in my enthusiasm, shouting them aloud.

"Heave!"

"Double!"

"Away!"

I felt the plane jerk forward, just as I had that morning, but this time I kept the stick in the central position.

In imagination, I now slid forward, keeping my direction and balancing so that neither wing dipped towards the ground. Then the plane came to a stop. I knew that I had carried out a faultless ground-slide . . .

I practiced a second and a third time and yet again for upwards of an hour, and then, calm and contented—and dead-tired, I went to sleep.

The next morning, after the alarm-clock had wrenched me mercilessly from sleep, I repeated, before getting up, the exercise of the night before. Then I set off again on my bicycle to Grunau.

So today I would be grounded. I had to put up with a good deal of harsh ridicule from my fellow pupils for the atmosphere on the course was a rough one, but although the experience was not pleasant, I have no doubt that it did me

good. At any rate, I felt absolutely certain in myself that
things would soon alter.

For the time being, after each ground slide, I was confined to helping the others load the glider on to a trailer and
haul it up the slope again. Throughout the day, there was
plenty to learn. I watched each slide attentively and seized
avidly on to each word of the instructor's criticism. In this
way, I quickly learnt where the mistakes lay and what had
been right or wrong in each pupil's handling of the plane.

That night, in bed I again practiced with the walking
stick noticing how much the experience I had gathered by
listening during the day now came to my assistance. I found
I could do ground slides quite easily, and now, in my
imagination, turned to carrying out little hops. When at last
I lay down to sleep, I did so in the happy feeling that I had
an instructive day behind me.

The second day of punishment, I again began with my
practices in bed. The previous evening, I had started to do
short hops. Today, I drew back the stick a fraction so that in
my imagination I could feel the plane take lightly off and
rise to about thirty or forty feet. I already felt quite sure of
myself and, again forgetting my surroundings, called out the
starting orders in a loud voice as I sat on my bed.

No wonder that my family gradually became alarmed
and that, in the brief moments when I was visible to them, I
found myself subjected to some anxious and questioning
glances.

The second day was little different from the first. I had to
help load up the glider after every slide and listened as Pit
van Husen criticised each pupil's performance.

A stroke of good fortune came to my assistance. As well as
our beginners course, an advanced course started at this
time, whose pupils, like "grown-up" fliers, took off from the
southern slope of the Galgenberg in an enclosed plane and
performed gliding flights, sometimes on a straight course, at
others executing prescribed turns. These pupils, to my joy,
had their lunch at a different time to ourselves, and while my
comrades sat down to their meal, I would creep away to

watch, full of envious longing, how the real flying was done.
As with us, every pupil in the advanced course received exact
instructions before he took off. It was all quite new to me.
So if—I repeated to myself—one wanted to turn to the left,
the ailerons and the rudder had also to be moved to the left.

That evening, in bed with my walking stick, I practiced
flying turns, sometimes flat, sometimes steep, but always
with a proper, clean carry-through. On the third day, I was
flying these turns in my imagination with as much confidence
as if I had had real experience and practice of flying. I was
filled with joy and even the jibes of my companions, which
were never lacking in Grunau, no longer had power to
affect me.

Thereafter, I was allowed to catch up with the others in
the work which I had missed. The ground slides were all
successful, each one better than the last, and I then went
over to hops, first short and then long ones. Soon I was on a
level with them once more.

Then came the day when a piece of great good fortune
befell me.

The first pupil on our course to be admitted to the "A"
Test was a plump, middle-aged man who had already flown
in the First World War as an observer and therefore had
more experience than the rest of us.

But today he had bad luck. When he tried to take off,
what with the lack of wind and his own weight, which was
considerable, the glider refused to leave the ground, however
strong an impetus his team tried to put into the start.

No wonder that the poor man became nervous and, zig-
zagging left and right, finally slithered ignominiously down
the slope. The rest of us followed whooping behind him to
haul the glider to the top again. At the starting point, Pit
van Husen then discussed with us the reasons for this failure.
Meanwhile, as a glider must never be left unweighted to be
blown about by the wind, he told me to seat myself in the
plane.

For the first time I was sitting now in a glider standing
some considerable way up the slope. Was not it as though I

was just waiting for the start? If, for example, I kept my eye
on that point there in the sky, I should certainly be able, if
required, to keep a straight course. If, then, I . . .

I now realised that for some time the others had been
watching me, laughing, among them the instructor. "All
right, harness up!" he said, thinking, no doubt, that from
that small height I could do nothing but a harmless slide.
The teams were already on the rope, the order rang out and
the glider rose slowly from the ground.

I noticed my speed, too good a speed for there to be any
point in trying to keep the plane to the ground. So holding
the stick lightly in my hands, I fixed my eyes on a spot on the
horizon in order to keep my course.

Then I looked right and left; thank God, the wings were
balanced and at last the dream I had cherished for years was
true and I was flying. Not for a single moment did I feel
insecure—my thought training was bearing its fruit.

But all good things come to an end and, the ground
approaching ever nearer as I lost height, I had at last to
land. I let the plane down in the prescribed fashion on the
meadow, slithered a little and then came to a stop, while the
left wing slowly tipped over on to the grass.

I did not stir, but simply sat there in my beloved glider,
caught in a blissful trance. With whoops and hoops my
comrades came running down from the starting site. For
thirty-nine seconds I had flown on a level course; the "A"
Test required only thirty seconds. The girl had been lucky,
shamelessly lucky! One might almost be jealous! But, of
course, it was the old story of the blind hen that manages
sometimes to pick up a grain of corn!

They could say what they liked, for I was filled with silent
joy at my experience. We loaded up the glider together and
pushed her up the slope. At the top, Pit van Husen was
waiting for us.

"I expect that was just luck. I can't count it for your "A"
Test."

Then, after a slight pause:

"You had better try it again, straight away."

I looked at him, unable to believe my ears. But I could see nothing to suggest he was joking. He must really mean it. The others had taken it that way, I could tell from their faces. So I made ready. Then a faint feeling of doubt entered my mind. Was I taking on too much . . . ?

But already the orders were ringing out and the glider rose once more into the air. Again I was flying.

I landed again in the prescribed fashion. "Huah—huah!" came from eighteen men's throats, as they ran down towards me. "Test passed," it meant, in Grunau language. "Hau, Boi," they called in Würtemberg, while in Rositten, they imitated the call of a crane . . .

That was only for advanced students, but this time it was also for me.

Next morning Wolf Hirth paid us a visit. He wanted to see for himself this girl who had so nearly come to grief at the very beginning and now, contrary to all expectation, had flown her "A" Test. He was tall and heavily built, had thick, dark hair, a high forehead and kind, rather mischievous eyes, now resting on me in quiet appraisal. To all flying pupils he was a demi-god.

Was it surprising that my heart beat up into my throat when he gave me the order to start? I had the same starting-site as the day before and was to land on the same meadow.

It may have pleased Wolf Hirth that I flew with such confidence but how that confidence had been acquired, I felt at the time hardly able to tell him!

On the following day, I was allowed, as a form of reward, to take off under his direction from a point higher up the slope, thereby increasing the length of the glide. After that, I flew every day under his personal supervision. He showed me how to fly turns, the S-turns which were required for the "B" Test, flat turns and steep turns and every time was amazed how I succeeded at the first attempt.

I did not dare to tell him at that time of my "training" in bed with the walking stick and I only realized myself its value much later, when I had to train young pilots in

Germany and abroad. I then realised that the best pilots are made by those who know best how to concentrate. I already possessed this faculty when I started my "training" in bed, thanks, principally, to my mother.

When I was a child of hardly six years old, regularly after the mid-day meal, my brother Kurt and I had been made to stretch ourselves out on the floor, place our hands behind our heads and, closing our eyes, try not to think of anything for five minutes on end, my mother sitting close by to supervise.

It was a continual mystery to me how such a feat could be achieved. Hardly would I close my eyes, than a literally endless succession of pictures and thoughts would chase through my head: my doll, that I had not washed, Kurt's toy railway, the tree in the garden that I planned to climb. Occasionally I would hazard a glance through half-closed lids at my brother lying beside me, then, seeing his eyes firmly closed, would quickly shut my own—to start all over again. Finally, when both resolution and will-power had failed, I would ask God if He would please help me to think of nothing. And every time we had to lie down on the floor, I would go on repeating this request, ceaselessly throughout the whole of the five minutes. One day, I confessed to my mother that my efforts to think of nothing never got beyond the stage of this endlessly repeated entreaty. To my amazement, she laughed heartily, advising me by all means to continue, and even though she was never able to make me relax completely, at least thanks to her I learnt how to concentrate on a definite object for a certain length of time.

My mother could never have guessed how useful this faculty was to become for me in later life.

After this course at the School of Gliding at Grunau, I returned to Rendsburg. Six months later, with a final examination, my schooling there came to an end.

And then the holidays lay before me once more, long and eagerly awaited holidays during which my father's permission for me to fly included my participation in a "C" Course at Grunau.

Again I pedalled out each day to the Galgenberg. We trained now on the southern slopes and beside the course instructor, Steinig, Wolf Hirth was also usually present.

In the first four days, there was an almost complete lack of wind,—time enough for us to practice S-turns, starting from high up the slope. Now we were no longer flying the open, primary training machines but, like real airmen, planes with an enclosed cockpit and fuselage. Needless to say, we were all not a little proud of this.

In our "C" Tests we were required to fly for at least five minutes in an up-wind above the level of our starting height.

But how, it may be asked, is it possible to maintain, let alone to increase one's height in a gliding plane that has no engine? Everyone must, at one time or another, have seen a motor-aircraft land. With its engine just ticking over, it glides slowly down, steadily losing height, towards the air-field. That seems obvious enough. It also seems obvious that a gliding plane that has had a catapulted take-off from some spot high up a mountain slope, will also inevitably glide down, like a motor aircraft with the engine turned off. How then from this process of gliding can height actually be gained?

In explanation, I will quote an example of Wolf Hirth's. Imagine an elevator in which a ladder is standing. I am perched on the topmost rung of the ladder and now gradually start to descend. As I do so, I begin to lose height. But if, at the same time, the elevator starts to ascend, I shall still reach the top floor, despite the fact that I have been climbing down the ladder.

In this example, I am the glider plane, losing height as it glides but nevertheless gaining in overall height because the up-wind, in other words, the elevator, is going up faster than I am coming down. Thus, although a plane when it is gliding invariably and continually loses in height, when it is in a fast-rising stream of air, it may be carried heigher than its original starting point.

This rising stream of air we call an "up-wind." How do up-winds occur? There are many different types but the simplest is the up-wind caused by a horizontal stream of air meeting and being deflected upwards by mountain or hill slopes or cliffs on the sea coast. In the case of a mountain, for example, the air flows up one side (Up-wind) and down the other (Down-wind).

If one takes off from a slope and keeps to the windward side, one can sail to and fro on the wind for as long as it blows and for as long as one has the energy to withstand the discomfort of a small, hard seat and the temptation to go to sleep.

To pass a "C" Test one must have luck with the weather. A "C" Course usually lasts no longer than a fortnight and if there happens to be no wind on any of the days, the pupils will have to go home without flying their Tests, for no amount of flying skill will avail them in dead calm weather.

But in our course we were lucky. Although there was almost no wind on the first few days, on the fifth day, it started to blow from the West. With Wolf Hirth and our instructor, Steinig, we climbed, full of joyous expectation, up the broad western slope of the Galgenberg to the starting site that lay about a hundred yards below the line of the ridge.

Here we stood by our machine, a group of grown men, of medium build, strong, hardened and weather-burnt, and among them, myself, small and slim, but like all of them, tense in every nerve.

Would I manage it? Would I be able to make use of the up-wind on the slope, keeping just the right speed, neither too fast nor too slow? And would the wind be strong enough or would I be forced to come down to the landing meadow in the valley? Would I be able to keep the right distance from the slope and not brush the trees before I was carried over the ridge? Would I crash the landing . . .?

Like a merry-go-round, the thoughts revolved in my head. Then I heard my name called and it was time to make ready.

I fetched my pillow—quite a fair-sized parcel—which I needed on account of my size and buckled the safety-belt. Then Wolf Hirth came up.

As soon as I was air-borne, I was to keep to the right, close,

but not too close, to the mountain side. I would soon feel the
lift of the wind.

How comforting it was to hear his clear, calm voice! Now,
surely, nothing could go wrong!

But there was much more I had to think of. Wolf Hirth
explained everything to me in detail.

I had to try and maintain the same, constant speed. On
reaching the far end of the slope, I had to turn through a
hundred-and-eighty degrees into the wind, to avoid being
carried over the ridge and so entering the down-wind where
I would quickly fall. I could stay up for five to ten minutes
and as a sign that it was time to land they were going to form
a chain on the starting-site. I was to land at the foot of the
West slope on the great landing meadow, just as I had learnt
in training.

The starting teams were standing by.

"All ready?"

"Heave!"

"Double!"

"Away!"

A short jerk, which pressed me back in my seat and I was
airborne.

The impetus carried me in a wide turn along the sides of
the slope. There were still bushes, pines and fir-trees above
me. But now I was to trust to the up-wind and cling to the
edge of the trees.

And suddenly, it was there! An invisible force lifted the
plane, thrusting me down in the cockpit. The up-wind now
carried me gently up the slope. I climbed higher and higher
and before I reached the far end, the ridge was already below
me. For the first time, I was flying like a bird!

As I made my first turn at the end of the slope, I hesitated.
Would I lose height or would the up-wind suffice to keep me
up? But all went better than I had hoped, and when I
executed my second turn above the starting-site, I was
already quite sure of myself.

The world looked strangely different from above. I was
only just over three hundred feet up but the figures below

already looked so small, I could no longer recognise their
faces.

There lay the southern slope with the glider hangar—and
there, like a toy model, the school and the village and, in the
distance, the lovely old town, with its familiar towers and
steeples. The world was beautiful almost beyond endurance . . .

Suddenly, I saw before me two buzzards, gliding with
motionless wings at the same height as myself. I knew that
where these birds were flying the up-wind would be at its
strongest.

I decided to follow them, my glider being somewhat faster
than they. Would they fly away as soon as I approached?

Already I could see the colour of each individual feather.
They kept their heads turned towards me, their eyes fixed on
the great, silent bird that was bearing me aloft. Why should
they flee before their big brother?

Carried by the wind, still soaring, they rose in the air, I
still striving to follow them. But they could do it better than
I and suddenly I found them far above me. Again the game
began. I flew after them, finding always a stronger up-wind
where they had been. So, in every nerve I strained to imitate
them, until my eye fell on my watch. Impossible that the ten
minutes given me by Wolf Hirth were already over! I looked
again. More than twenty minutes had passed. Perhaps my
watch was wrong. I could tell by looking at the starting-site,
where they were going to form a chain when it was time to
land. And there they were—waving up at me! How long had
they been there? No use fright seizing me in every limb, I
would quickly have to come down to land.

Not only had I incurred, for the second time, the reproach
of being disobedient and undisciplined, I would certainly
have deprived another pupil of the chance of taking off today
for his "C" Test and who could tell whether there would be
wind again tomorrow? To haul the glider from the landing-
ground to the starting-site would take a good half-hour, even
if a horse were available to pull the trailer. How would it be
if I landed, then, directly on the starting-site? There was

plenty of room. It would only need to be carefully thought
out so that I did not come to grief by sliding over the edge
of the site.

Cautiously I dropped into the down-wind, still leaving
myself the possibility of reaching the up-wind side of the
slope. In this way, I quickly lost height. Then, at a moderate
height above the landing-site, I allowed myself to be driven
back by the wind, putting the nose down towards the ground
at what seemed to me the correct moment, and then, the
ground coming up at great speed, flattened out at the last
moment with a gentle pull on the stick, to touch down at the
edge of the site and slide forward, still at considerable speed,
and halt at the very spot I had selected. And the plane was
intact! I was breathless for joy!

It was lucky for me that I had not been able to hear the
potent curses that Wolf Hirth had shouted into the wind as
already in imagination he saw me crash to the ground. But
now he was no less relieved than I that all had gone well and
before I finally stood before him, his anger had already
given place to joy at my happy landing. So now he was very
indulgent, merely tweaking me lightly by the ear as he told
me: "I ought really to be angry with you for acting against
instructions,—and as a warning to the rest of you, I will
repeat here and now: anyone who acts in future in this way
without first obtaining permission, will be grounded at once.
We must have discipline here."

Then: "From the flying point of view, of course, the performance was perfect . . ."

Can I be blamed if the rest of the day seemed to pass in a
blaze of sunshine?

Some days later, I was to realise that my flight had, after
all, given him pleasure. The pride of the school was a new
plane, that only Wolf Hirth and the instructors were
allowed to fly. But for me he made an exception and I was
the first pupil to obtain permission to fly it, staying up for as
long as I liked and the wind conditions would allow.

For the first time, I was now free to fly without restrictions
and I took off with feelings of real pride to soar for as long as

the winds would blow, drawing on the loveliest songs I
could remember and singing them aloud into the sky, hardly
noticing that it rained and snowed and coming down only
when after five hours the wind finally expired.

Thankful, as always when things had gone well, I touched
down—to be greeted by an excited throng of people, con-
gratulating me on a world record.

That evening the news was given on the radio, while
flowers and messages of congratulation poured in on my
parents at home.

As for me, I found it wonderful—I was young and I was
overjoyed. But that evening when I retired, on my bed was a
letter from my mother. "Do you realise with gratitude," she
wrote, "that it is the grace of good fortune that has brought
you this success?"

"What does that mean?" I thought rebelliously. "Grace
of good fortune?" Snow, wind, rain and cold I had had to
withstand and the pain and agony of a pitilessly hard seat.
What could my mother know about flying?

But the longer I thought, the more I had to agree that she
was right. "Good fortune": was not the wind that had kept
up throughout the day a part of it?

I began to see that it is good fortune that crowns all undertakings with success, and in this light I looked, next day, at
the presents and flowers which were still arriving for me at
home.


### 3.  From Gliding to Powered Flight

EVER SINCE that experience, I have been in love with
flying. I went to Berlin for my first term as medical
student, attended the first lectures and all the while had only
one desire—to fly again!

In my letters to my parents I managed to convince them
that for my career as flying doctor in Africa it would be

necessary for me to learn to pilot engined aircraft and, although they were by no means happy at the thought of my doing so, they were sufficiently impressed by the seriousness of my intentions to give their agreement in principle.

Their love and understanding were such that they could never wish to prevent me from making my own life but, anxious lest I should fall a prey to superficial ambition, they confronted me with the hard necessity of having to pay for the training course myself out of the money which they had allowed me for my expenses as medical student.

At that time, the German Air Mails ran three amateur flying schools, in Berlin-Staaken, in Würzburg and in Stuttgart-Böblingen. I contacted the School in Staaken and entered my name for a course in flying sports planes.

Each day of the course I would set off at 5 a.m. to bicycle to Staaken, in the western suburbs of Berlin. At first I was the only girl pupil, the others being men of all ages, merchants, engineers, chemists, journalists and the actor Mathias Wiemann, with whom I soon formed a real flying friendship. Many of them arrived in their own cars and practiced flying as a pastime, looking on it as a pleasant form of social relaxation. On days when there was no flying they were therefore well content to sit chatting in the restaurant of the clubhouse. On these occasions I would be the cuckoo-in-the-nest, preferring to spend my time in the workshops, where there was much to learn: the aircraft engines, for example,—a new, strange world!

I soon realised that it meant little to be able to fly a powered plane, that was quickly learnt. But if a pilot knew nothing about the engine, he was ignorant of the very heart of his machine; I made up my mind therefore that I would learn everything there was to know about it.

The ground mechanics in the workshops were mostly middle-aged men with long experience and they did not exactly welcome the intrusion of flying pupils who got in the way and interrupted their work with innumerable silly questions, and being totally ignorant of mechanics I hardly knew, even, what questions to ask.

So at first I had to overcome a certain shyness, but I was determined not to allow myself to be overawed and I continued to badger them, poking into all I could see, until I could say that I had grasped the first principles and was beginning to understand each time now more and more about the mechanics of an aircraft engine. In return for all I was learning, I helped to polish the aircraft.

One day, I was given my first job of work to do. The foreman mechanic was a quiet, modest man but a great expert and he had decided to see whether anything had sunk in of what he had had to tell that stupid little girl with her incessant questions. He also wanted to see whether I would shirk hard work and dirt. I had therefore, at first under his supervision, to dismantle an old aircraft engine that was unfit for use. Then, on the Sunday, when there was no one about, I had to try and put it together again.

That sounds much easier than I found it, at that time. I knew that my only chance of succeeding was to proceed completely systematically and when dismantling I made countless drawings and sketches, like a medical student at a dissection, so that when it came to reassembling the motor, I should be able to recognise each individual component.

Without a break, I worked that Sunday and on through the following night, until on the Monday morning, with torn and bleeding hands and covered from head to foot in oil and grime, I was able to show the foreman the reassembled engine.

He said little, merely nodding in approval, and neither did the men who were standing round or came later, one by one, during the day to have a look at the job, but from that time on I was no longer looked upon as a "fair-weather flyer" and was accepted as one of them.

Thereafter I took every opportunity of getting to know the different types of aircraft engine, I read all the technical literature I could lay my hands on and went on learning continually and without pause.

It occurred to me that it would be no disadvantage for me to be able to drive a car and know something about motor

engines. Naturally no owner was going to allow an ignora-
mus like myself to drive his car and so it seemed impossible
to learn without attending a School of Motoring. But that
would require money,—money I had not got.

Eventually, however, I found a solution. Each time I took
off from Staaken, I had noticed a gang of workmen engaged
in transporting loads of rubble, by means of tractor and
trailer, along the road flanking the airfield. We used to wave
to each other as I passed over their heads. One day I so
arranged matters that, after flying, when the other pupils
had returned to the club-house, my way led me past these
workers—and we quickly came into conversation.

One of them had an eye complaint: I promised to ask my
father to send some ointment for him. Another came from
Silesia. A third wanted to know who the girl was who
waved to them every day from her plane! At first I evaded
the question and listened, secretly contented, as they expressed their amazement at a girl learning to fly. Apparently,
they were greatly impressed and, like most people who have
never done it, thought flying must be a very difficult and
dangerous task. At last I had to tell them that I was the girl.
They were now even more impressed and bombarded me
with questions about every detail of my training. Meanwhile, I was helping to load the rubble on to the trailer and
before we had finished, we were already good friends.

So I took courage and though I had not the faintest idea
what to do with the clutch pedal or the gears, I asked if they
would let me drive the tractor. Laughing, they agreed. At
first, of course, I stalled the engine but I quickly discovered
how it should be done and then drove the tractor to the far
end of the field, tipped off the rubble and drove back to
them in triumph. From then on, they let me drive the tractor
every day—my self-imposed task and my secret joy—and so
it was almost as a game that I learnt to drive, without paying
a cent.

My new friends were all excellent types and had to work
hard to earn their wage. Almost all had been through hard
times, many being unemployed for long periods, and as they

talked, I realised how fortunate I myself had been. The older ones had been through the First World War, you could tell it from their faces and their scars. After doing their duty for years in the trenches, they had returned home to be insulted and spat upon and have the shoulder-straps torn by hooligans from their uniforms. It was no wonder that their experiences had made them very embittered. ". . . Just as if it was us who had been the trouble-makers," they said, almost in self-defence, "—as if it was a positive pleasure to stop a Lewis-gun bullet . . ."

I acquired a deep insight into their trials and tribulations. I shared with them the food parcels from home—I got my mother to send a dress or two for their wives—and I was happy in their company.

But as soon as the men began to talk politics, our good relations threatened to be disturbed. In the whole gang there were hardly two who belonged to the same party and with horror I realised how people who otherwise get on well together can become bitter and fanatical opponents as soon as politics are mentioned. It was all new to me, for though naturally I had been brought up to be a patriot, there had never been any question of political divisions in my home.

Inevitably, each of the men tried to win me over to his views and one day so fierce an argument developed between them that they almost came to blows. Then, depressed and thoughtful, I left them, for our happy atmosphere seemed now finally to have been destroyed.

Meanwhile, I had made progress with my flying, learning easily and without effort in a training plane fitted with duel controls. To start with, our instructor, Otto Thomsen, accompanied me. He taught in a hard school and some of the things he shouted at me during our flights were not exactly endearing. But he was an excellent teacher and I soon realised that only by the hard way can one learn to be a safe and competent pilot. That I had not, after all, made so bad an impression on him became clear when, after only a few flights together, he took the unusual step of allowing me to fly alone.

Once again, I was on the fringe of a new world, this time, not the vast and soundless world of gliding but a world narrowed to a small strip of sky lying between me and the earth and filled with the throb and thunder of the engine. For I was still flying in our open Mercedes-Klemm at quite low altitudes and the earth still seemed to be within my reach and I, still to be its child. How it smiled up at me as I flew over it, how the trees held out their arms, their topmost branches waving like the outstretched fingers of a hand!

But then came the day—that day when my workmen friends had begun to quarrel—when I was to take off for my altitude test and, for the first time, slip from the earth's embrace.

I was allowed two hours flying time in which to reach a height of 6,500 feet and our good old "Klemm," already a trifle lame, with its modest twenty horse-power would require a good hour to attain that height. In a fur-lined flying suit, my face greased for protection against sun and cold, I climbed into the plane. Before the take-off, I had to listen to a deal of good advice, for the sky, which had hitherto been a cloudless blue, was now rapidly becoming overcast and I was therefore to break off the flight in good time, should conditions seem to require it.

I listened carefully while I was briefed, but though surrounded by a group of people, I had the strange feeling that I was no longer one of them. Potent, yet gentle, like some seductive wine, the fever of flying descended on me, coursing through me to my very finger-tips.

At last, I was allowed to open the throttle and taxi over the field. I rose into the air, flying over the group of workmen. Were they still arguing about politics? I had little time to think of that, for my ear was concentrated on the engine, ready to note the least interruption in its quiet rhythm and my eyes were fixed on the instrument panel, checking temperature and revolutions.

First I flew a wide turn over the airfield, then I started to climb, higher and higher, 900 feet, 1,200 feet—1,500 feet, and at each stage, more towns and villages, more woods and fields and meadows surged over the horizon to meet me. I saw Berlin, sprawled like a giant below, then shrinking to Lilliputian size, the cars darting hither and thither like a swarm of restless midges.

So I climb up, my eyes still riveted on the earth, still seeking to identify and to recognise. But now all merges into anonymity, into oblongs, squares and brilliant patches of colour. As though pained at parting, I still gaze towards the ground, but soon the earth below dwindles into insignificance and then my eyes turn up to meet the vast and solitary expanses of the sky. At last and for the first time, I am alone.

Soon the scene changes again and legions of little cloud balls are sailing past me. They look so solid that I am afraid to touch them and they are moving continually, all around me, swirling up, swelling and dissolving again. Yet the spaces between them are so large that I can rise above them as though passing through broad valleys. I have never been so high before and from here, glimpsed through the rifts in the clouds, the earth seems like some distant island, fretted with foaming surf.

At great altitudes, the airman feels close to God. All that hitherto seemed important falls away. Pride, whether of name, position or calling, dissolves into humility, while the fume of Earth evaporates, leaving the mind clear and quiet, at one with Creation, happy—and thankful.

When I landed again at Staaken, I was still under the influence of this experience, though none of those who spoke to me or congratulated me could have guessed my thoughts. For many days thereafter, I noticed how everything in me seemed to be in rebellion against the normal routine of life, for there was no part of it that did not now seem to me boundlessly trivial and empty.

But I recognised soon enough the inner danger to which I was exposed. In the life of every airman there comes a turning-point when, having experienced the sublimity of great altitudes, he either seeks to become worthy of the vision which has been granted to him, or else turns to boastful arrogance, casting aside all restraint or respect, respect, even, towards God. Sensing this, I wrote at that time to my mother: "I will and must bring myself to go about Berlin without thinking continually of flying. Otherwise I shall never again be able to learn how to stand with both feet on the ground."

As the training course continued at Staaken, my fellow pupils and I came to be on very good terms. Among them were several Chinese, friendly and courteous people for whom we all had a high regard. But they had one habit which annoyed me—among themselves they always spoke Chinese, of which we others understood not a word. So, one day, in order to embarrass them, I told them that I could understand their language and, in proof, took it upon myself to sing to them a Chinese song which my father had taught us when we were children. I sang and sang happily on, without noticing that they were indeed embarrassed, so much so that none of the German bystanders could possibly fail to notice it.

When I had finished, the Chinese were naturally pressed to tell us the reason, which, it was clear, had something to do with the song. Their explanation caused a roar of laughter and even greater embarrassment to myself, for the text of the song had consisted of nothing but a string of street-corner swear words!

My father had heard these expressions in the streets of Pekin and later had put them together for us children in order to amuse us with the strange sounding words,—naturally never imagining that we would ever discover their meaning. So that we could learn them more easily, he had set them to the tune of a well-known Chinese song.

When I told him of my performance, it caused him something of a shock and I feel sure that he took good care never to repeat this linguistic experiment for the benefit of his grand-children.

In my medical studies I had done nothing during the whole of that term. I had hardly attended a single lecture and though, indeed, I had strapped my text books on to my bicycle when I rode out each morning to Staaken, that was usually as far as they got. My flying activities, I found, left hardly any time for study.

As soon as the vacation began, I went home, intending to spend all that I could of the summer in flying.

I was no longer required to take part in a training course, but there was still an enormous amount for me to learn and here, to my great good fortune, Wolf Hirth took me under his fatherly wing. He and his wife had become friendly with my parents and fully agreed with them that, while being allowed to perfect my skill as a pilot, I should continue with my medical studies with the object of becoming a doctor. Flying was not a career.

It was Wolf Hirth who initiated me into the "High School of Soaring" and I gratefully acknowledge that the instruction which he gave me during those months formed the basis of my whole flying career. A young man who had devoted himself heart and soul to the art of flying, no one could have been better suited than he to impart the fruits of flying experience and it is rightly that he is looked upon today as the patriarch of gliding. Not only has he committed to writing, for the benefit of all future gliding pupils, the very smallest details of his vast experience and knowledge, but he is himself a masterly flier, overcoming by sheer force of will the twofold impediments of short-sightedness and an artificial limb. Among other great achievements, he was the first ever to fly over New York in a glider, a feat which he performed in 1931.

The instruction which I now received from him in the theory of soaring took place in the most practical manner. Wolf Hirth had just been sent for correction the proofs of his book on the High School of Long Distance Soaring and he allowed me to help him in his task, encouraging me to ask questions on anything which I did not understand. In this way, while I learned, he discovered whether his book would be readily grasped by his younger readers.

But he had not forgotten my parents' anxiety for me not to

neglect my medical studies and he now set me a task. Since the loss of his leg, he had come to concern himself with the anatomy of the thigh and the knee-joint, about which he possessed extensive knowledge. On this subject I was now told to prepare an oral lecture and until I had delivered it to him, there was to be no flying.

How restlessly my heart beat when I heard the weather forecast predict strong westerly winds for the following day; I thought I would hardly be able to control my yearning! But I knew that Wolf Hirth had been in deadly earnest and to ensure a day's flying for myself on the morrow there seemed no alternative: I would have to prepare my lecture that very night.

On the pretext of going early to bed, I shut myself in my room, took out my books and read and learnt and read again until I thought I had done enough.

Early next morning when I got up, I could see outside my windows the trees bending before the wind and ragged clouds skeltering across the sky,—perfect weather for gliding! Whatever happened, I decided, I would have to reach Wolf Hirth and deliver my lecture before he left his home for Grunau.

I had never jumped so quickly out of bed and just before seven I was at his door breathlessly explaining my call to his astonished wife. I had hardly finished when Wolf Hirth, still in his dressing gown, appeared in the doorway and heard what I wanted. Laughing, he pushed me into his study, telling me to wait there until he was ready to leave.

What a room! I stood as if transfixed. Everything, yes,— everything was here that an airman's heart could wish for, models of gliders, illustrating the development of the different types, and all round the room wherever one looked, picture upon picture of gliding, the clouds seeming so real, I almost felt I was flying. And there was much more in the room besides—cups which Wolf Hirth had won flying, or, earlier, in motor-cycle racing, mementoes of foreign lands and whole shelves and cupboards full of books and magazines on flying—a treasure-trove for me and for any flying pupil

who might find his way here. I hardly knew where I should
start reading; I was interested in everything.

But soon, too soon, Wolf Hirth appeared and we set off
together in his car for Grunau. During the journey he
suggested I should give my lecture on the knee-joint, so, to
divert his thoughts, I quickly asked him to explain to me
some of the things I had been reading in his flying books,
and before long, we were buried in our flying problems and
my medical lecture was completely forgotten. Arrived in
Grunau, I was then allowed to spend the whole of the
morning flying—my night's vigil had been in vain!

Wolf Hirth seemed to have dismissed all thought of
medicine from his head, for now he engaged me as one of
his assistants in the workshop in constructing and repairing
gliders and occasionally, as a reward, when the weather was
fine, he allowed me to fly.

After each day's work, I would spend the evening with the
Hirths. The three of us would sit in the study, his wife with
her sewing, Wolf Hirth writing or painting and myself
sitting on the carpet, surrounded by galley-proofs, magazines
and books on flying for which there had been no room on
any of the shelves.

I asked innumerable questions and tirelessly Wolf Hirth
answered them, explaining what I did not understand. For
me at this particular time, this manner of learning was a
piece of great good fortune, how great I was only to realise
later when I saw how it had saved me years of learning by
trial and error.

My experiences in gliding at that time were confined to
exploiting the type of up-wind which is caused by air-
currents striking an obstacle, for example a mountain slope,
and being deflected upwards. Wonderful though the
experience is of gliding in this way, the scope is always
limited, even when it is possible to fly from one slope to
another. With the slope-wind, it is never possible to soar to
great heights or over long distances.

Until the year 1926, wherever gliding was practiced

throughout the world, only this one type of up-wind was understood. Since then, many further types have been explored, among them the "thermal," enabling soaring to reach hitherto undreamed-of achievements. The book by Wolf Hirth was a summary of the experiences obtained to-date in this field.

These "thermals" occur over places where the ground has been warmed unevenly by the sun. On days when the summer sun has been shining, everyone will have noticed how dry areas such as heath, roads or sand warm up more quickly than damp, low-lying areas.

This difference in the temperature of various stretches of ground is repeated in the temperature of the air above them and thus a clearly defined movement is set up in the atmosphere, the warmer regions of air rising faster than the cooler ones adjacent to them. These rising convection currents, or "thermals," usually vary in diameter from three hundred to six hundred feet.

The position of thermals can often be detected by the bunches of cumulus cloud which are seen hovering above them. As the stream of air in the thermal rises, it becomes cooler, condensing its moisture into millions of minute droplets, so light that they hover in the air, appearing to us in the form of small, shiny cloud-balls. These are the glider pilot's signposts to the thermals.

As the thermals are limited in area, the pilot can only stay in them by circling continually, as though he were enclosed in the flue of a gigantic chimney. Here the buzzards and the falcons come to his aid and as soon as he sees one wheeling upwards in a thermal, he follows, keeping as close to it as he can. These birds can reach great heights simply by circling with outstretched wings and they are far more sensitive to changes in air pressure than the human being, whose eardrum can only detect wide differences in altitude.

But as the assistance of buzzards or falcons is not always available, the glider pilot is provided with another aid, the instrument—indispensable in gliding—known as the Variometer, which records the rate of increase or decrease in barometric pressure and hence the rate of climb or descent of the aircraft.

I became acquainted with the whole subject of thermal flying by studying the proofs of Wolf Hirth's book and in conversation with him during those evenings I naturally absorbed the knowledge almost without effort. I then began to long for the day when I would be able to gather experience of thermals for myself. So there began for me a firm friendship with Wolf Hirth and his wife and thenceforward they looked on me as their "flying child."

Every evening, at an agreed time, my parents came to fetch me from the Hirths. At first, no doubt, they were at a loss to explain the strange and powerful spell which flying had laid upon me. But they were loving and wise enough not to oppose me in my course and they tried to follow me as best they could, learning more and more about my wonderful new world in the conversations which we had together, lasting often far into the night. To them I confided all my interests and hopes and, here again, it was above all my mother who never flagged or faltered in her understanding and encouragement.

## 4. Medical Student at Kiel University

FOR MY second term as medical student, my father wanted me to go to Kiel University. He himself had studied there for a time and the Medical Faculty had an excellent reputation, my brother was stationed in Kiel as a midshipman in the Kriegsmarine and, moreover, there were hardly any sport facilities in winter time which might distract me from my studies.

At the time my father entered my name, I did not know, however, that the Medical Faculty at this particular university was so overcrowded that, before being permitted to attend dissections, second term students were required to furnish proof of an adequate knowledge of anatomy in an oral examination.

I only heard this at the very end of the holidays when arrangements for my departure had already been made and it was too late for me to catch up on my studies—the news, therefore, came as a considerable shock. I decided that there was only one thing to do, go to another, less crowded university. I told my parents and I explained to them the reasons, but they simply did not believe me. A degree of ignorance such as I claimed to possess was beyond their power to conceive. In vain I protested, in vain I spoke to each of them alone. The result was always the same: I would manage to pass if only I had confidence in my knowledge.

The situation seemed hopeless. The neglect of my studies during my first term now lay on me like a ton-weight—that first term in which I had not once opened a book. I could have made up for lost time if only my parents had been open to my attempts at persuasion. That they had not believed me, showed how much I had abused their confidence and their goodness in making it possible for me to fly.

I knew that to go to Kiel would be a journey wasted, for me, but not from my parents' point of view because, whatever happened, they wished me to sit for the examination.

Dejected and feeling very small, I sat in the train to Kiel. All seemed vista'd in gloom. The rain spattered down on the windows, the clouds were sagging almost to the ground. During the journey, I had time enough for reflection. In imagination, I saw myself already in the crowded examination hall, heard my name called and felt the hostile, searching eyes of the examiner upon me as I failed to answer a single one of his questions. Even supposing he were well disposed and tried, at first, to suggest some of the answers, he would be bound finally, either to take me for a mental case, or else, amid the mocking laughter of the students, order me angrily from the hall. The mere thought of it made me go hot and cold . . .

I decided I would stay away from the examination, then I

realised, it would be no good; I would not only destroy my parents' faith in me, I would also compel them to think me a coward.

I would have to turn up for the examination—so much was decided. I would have to take the consequences of my own neglect. I had deserved the punishment, now I would have to accept it. Perhaps Heaven intended it as a salutory lesson, because hitherto I had succeeded too easily. I would look at the inevitable from the positive side, would try to turn it to my gain. To bear the shame worthily seemed to me now more important than passing the examination. I had long known that all growth is accompanied by pain.

That thought sufficed to calm me for the rest of the day, but when, next morning, I stood in the foyer of the hall amid a sea of students, all, I imagined, about to take the examination, my nerve again threatened to desert me. Wherever I turned, I heard talk of the examination, likely subjects were trumpeted about, concepts were blazoned forth and never, in my life before, had I heard of any of them. My courage seemed to turn to water. Would it not be better, after all, if I . . .?

I crept quietly to the door, from where I could see the broad sky. I took a deep breath and thought of my altitude flight in Staaken, when the earth, with all its worries and cares had seemed to fall away beneath me. As I did so, everything in me seemed to become calm again and I imagined myself flying higher and higher into the deepening blue. What matter if I were put to shame? What reason had I to be ashamed at all?

My courage returned and I went into the examination hall. The ordeal began. The first student stepped forward to the rostrum and the Professor proceeded to question him. Some of his answers were right, others were wrong and the latter were quickly seized on and thrown as an entertaining morsel to the onlookers. The atmosphere seemed to me intolerable. The first was completely failed. The second quickly lost his nerve and I could feel his distress almost physically.

And so the agony continued, until I suddenly heard my own name called. At that moment, I felt calm and assured again; though I would be sure to fail, it no longer seemed to matter and I stepped forward to the rostrum.

On a table beside the Professor lay a pile of human bones. The examinee was first told the parts of the body on which he was to be questioned and then to select the relevant bones from the pile, using them to illustrate his answers to the subsequent questions. That would be catastrophe Number One!

Professor B. looked at me encouragingly. Apparently he interpreted my calm as the confidence born of knowledge. "With you," his look seemed to say, "I can see it will be different." If only he knew!

"You will take the region of the thigh."

I could hardly believe my ears. The thigh was the one subject which I had learnt that night for my lecture to Wolf Hirth. Perhaps something of it would have stuck in my mind.

But would I be able to recognise the thigh-bone? I supposed it ought to be the largest. But—perhaps they had put in a child's thigh-bone, as a trick?

Professor B. held it to be a sheer impossibility for anyone not to recognise the thigh-bone. So he went to the table, searched among the pile of bones and handed one to me:

"It ought not to be difficult to find *that* bone."

I nodded, beaming—then asked for a few minutes' reflection. Then I began to recount what I knew, speaking slowly and clearly in order to gain time, diluting my account, here and there, with some information about the knee-joint. When Professor B. tried to interrupt me, I carried calmly on, as though I had not heard him. Thereby I quickly had the laughers on my side, without allowing them to confuse me.

But sooner or later, my fate would overtake me. My lecture for Wolf Hirth contained nothing about the ligaments surrounding the bone and I knew only one, the "ligamentum ileofemorale." Therefore I ended my dissertation at the point where this ligament began, so as to suggest it as the next question. And the question came and my answer followed, so swift and sure, that it served as further proof of the solidity of my knowledge. As for me, I knew only that I knew no more. Now, surely, the blow would fall?

I waited. Then I heard the Professor say:

"Correct, the ileofemorale. I see that your knowledge is adequate. Good,—passed."

For a moment I stood as if paralysed and almost gave myself away. Then I went back to my place, hardly daring to look to right or to left.

I telegraphed the result to my parents. They wired back: "We knew you would." They could not have guessed how greatly these words depressed me, for I had made use of their goodness and generosity in allowing me to fly, but their trust I had thoughtlessly abused.

## 5. My First Flight in a Storm-Cloud

MAY, 1933. Home again to Hirschberg for the holidays —the countryside still wrapped in the splendour of spring, the peaks of the Riesengebirge still in their snowy mantles. Everywhere on trees and bushes the buds are beginning to burst and the air is sweetly soft and warm. Wonderful weather for gliding! As I walk through the sun-drenched streets of Hirschberg, I am yearning to soar up into the blue, gleaming sky, veiled only here and there by a happy-seeming cloud of purest white.

Suddenly, as though in answer to my wish, there is a screech of brakes and a car jerks to a stop beside me. A well-known voice speaks a greeting in my ear,—Wolf Hirth! He and his wife are going to Grunau for a short flight to take some ciné films of Hirschberg from the air, and I may come with them to be towed up in the "Grunau Baby," the very latest type of training glider,—just as I am, in my light summer dress, with short stockings and sandals! But what

does it matter? There is hardly a cloud in the sky, there will
be very little bumpiness, though perhaps somewhere I shall
be able to find a faint up-wind.

An hour later, I am sitting in the cabin of my glider, without goggles or helmet, the parachute harness buckled straight
over my frock.

Wolf Hirth tells me to try flying blind, by instruments only
and, as far as possible, not let my eyes stray outside the
cabin.

In the evenings I had spent with Wolf Hirth, I had learnt
that a pilot is deprived of his vision, not only at night but also
when flying through cloud.

I have already mentioned that up-winds are usually to be
found under cumulus cloud. Even stronger up-winds are
encountered inside the cloud itself, particularly in storm
clouds. In the latter, the wind can reach a vertical speed of
130 to 160 feet per second and any aircraft caught in it is
pulled upward with gigantic force. Such violent turbulence
can be a danger to any type of plane, particularly when
accompanied by thunder storms, hail or icing-up. Moreover,
when in cloud, an airman is unable to determine the attitude
of his plane in relation to the horizon, the human organs of
equilibrium being inadequate to convey to us our "absolute
position in space."

I had learnt that in cloud his instruments are the pilot's
most important aid. In those days the chief of these was the
Turn-and-Slip Indicator. Theoretically I had often practiced blind-flying, using a well known and simple aid. I drew
on separate pieces of cardboard about playing-card size all
the combinations of readings—there are nine in all—which
the Turn-and-Slip Indicator and the Cross-Level could
show for different positions of the aircraft. I made a habit of
carrying these cards with me pulling one out in a spare
moment to test my knowledge, thus:

Indicator right—Cross-Level central:
a normal right-handed turn.
Indicator right—Cross-Level left:
a flat, skidding turn with not enough bank.

At first, when faced with a card, I had to think for the answer and as long as this was necessary, I considered myself unfit to cope with an emergency. Thought, I argued to myself, has a habit of "cutting-out" in moments of danger and therefore an immediate, purely mechanical reaction is essential if the right action is to be taken in time. So I continued my daily practice with the cards until I could translate completely automatically the instrument readings on each into the movements required to control the plane.

As Wolf Hirth towed me up in my glider, I therefore felt quite confident that I should be able to fly "blind" without getting into difficulties.

At about 1,200 feet, Wolf gave me the signal to cast off and as soon as I had done so, I began to lose height, gliding softly and swiftly down without the faintest breath of an up-current anywhere. Now I was no more than 250 feet up and was fast nearing the earth.

I was already looking for a suitable spot to land when suddenly the glider began to quiver. What did this mean, up-current, or down-current? Then I saw that the pointer of the Variometer stood a little over zero at "Climb."

I now began to circle, maintaining my height and even increasing it a little. Then, once more, I suddenly dropped. I searched round for the up-current and found, instead, a different one, much stronger. Again I climbed, this time very fast. The Variometer started at 1½ feet per second, then rose to 3, then 6, then 9 feet per second, and still it went on rising, faster and faster. I had never experienced this kind of thing before.

I went on circling up and up till, before I knew what was happening, I had risen a further 1,500 feet, in about two-and-a-half minutes.

And now, quite involuntarily, my eyes turned from the instruments to the sky. Immediately overhead stood a gigantic black cloud: it must have formed only in the last few minutes. A more practiced eye would, of course, have discovered it long ago, but I had acted strictly according to Wolf Hirth's instructions and had kept my gaze riveted the whole time on my instruments, so as not to be tempted to judge the attitude of the plane by the horizon.

At any rate, the sight of this dark monster filled me with glee. Here, at last, was the opportunity of an experience I had been longing for, to fly through a cloud. Without an inkling of the real danger of my situation, I was still absolutely confident, pinning my faith on my knowledge of the instruments, and had not Wolf Hirth himself told me that as long as he has that knowledge, a pilot can come to no harm?

So, surging ever higher, here I sit, 3,000 feet, and higher still to 3,600 feet,—and now, I break in at the base of the cloud, the first dark wisps brush past me and I take a farewell look at the solid world. I have just time to see a last tiny fragment before a thick white veil suddenly drops, shutting me tightly in, alone with my cloudy company . . .

With eager concentration, I rivet my gaze on the instruments. Afraid? No, not in the least! I am as confident as confident can be—more confident than I shall ever be in any sort of a cloud again.

And still I am climbing, faster and faster, at twenty feet a second, now. Is the cloud, perhaps, slowly approaching the peaks of the Riesengebirge, there to deposit me on the Schneekoppe, the topmost peak of all? A second's thought, and I am reassured. My own height is now 5,500 feet, but the Schneekoppe is only 5,200 feet—so all is well and I am out of danger. I take a deep breath of relief, little suspecting what is yet to come . . .

And then,—a million drum-sticks suddenly descend on the glider's wings and start up, in frenzied staccato, an ear-splitting, hellish tattoo, till I am dissolved and submerged in fear. Through the windows of the cabin, which are already icing up, I can see the storm cloud spewing out rain and hail. I take some time to bring my fear under control, but when I have repeated to myself often enough that this, after all, is a perfectly normal natural phenomenon and can see as well from the evidence of my instruments that the plane is in the correct attitude of flight, I become calmer again.

Soon, indeed, the drumming ceases, but in the conflicting

air currents, the wings are alternately lifted and depressed and, thrown about from corner to corner of my cabin, I have a hard struggle to make my instruments continue reading as the text-book says they should. And all the while, the glider is still climbing, 8,500 feet—9,100, nine thousand seven hundred and fifty feet above the earth.

What I now see, I simply cannot bring myself to believe— the instruments seem to be sticking. They move still, but more and more slowly till, finally, they cease to move at all and not all my blows and buffets will bring them to life again. They are stuck, because they are frozen solid.

I try to hold the control column in the normal position, but it is a hopeless task, for,—what is the normal position? With my instruments useless, I cannot tell . . . Now there is nothing left that I can do.

. . . There is a new sound, a kind of high-pitched whistle, now loud, now soft. As soon as it stops, I know I must put the nose down quickly, for that will be the moment when the plane has reached the stall. But now, as I suddenly pitch forward, helpless, in my harness and the blood shoots painfully into my head, I know that the moment has already passed.

The plane must be diving vertically and have swung over almost on to its back.

Then it swings forward again and plunges down at immense speed in a headlong dive.

I heave at the stick and heave and go on heaving (quite unaware that I am performing a series of involuntary loops), —and again I suddenly find myself hanging in my harness, while the glider arrows down, shrieking . . .

The mica window of the cabin has long ago frosted over and now, rather than be shut in any longer, powerless and alone, I break a hole in it with my fist. At least I shall be able to see.

Now I am shivering, all over, in every tissue of my body, and my bare hands turn blue as, nearly ten thousand feet above the earth, in my summer frock, I sit, basking in rain, hail and snow, my streaming hair tossed like seaweed in a storm.

The plane no longer answers to the controls and, in any case, is probably better left now to its own devices. So, hoping faintly that its inherent stability may suffice to avert disaster, I abandon the stick. As I do so, no longer the pilot now, but a passenger, I feel the fear inside me suddenly lift and creep a pace nearer my heart.

The tempest has now mounted to an inferno. Helpless as a shuttle, I am thrown ceaselessly to and fro in the cockpit, unable to stretch my feet to the control pedals, unable, even to clench my teeth, now the gale has wedged open my jaws.

. . . And the glider is climbing again—already, my eyes are straining out of their sockets. Soon, I know, the blood will spurt from my temples . . . And the fear lifts on its haunches for another spring. My brain is drained almost empty, the last shreds of thought flit through it, like leaves across an autumn sky.

How long to go before she breaks up, till I can bale out? Wolf Hirth, Hirth,—what did he say? "Everyone knows fear sometime—if alone, then talk to yourself, aloud—*loud*—"
"HANNA-A—!" I scream, "Ya! Ya-a! Coward! Hang on, can't you, cowa-ar—!"

Listen! I thought I heard a voice,—yes, there! Very faint, thin, but a human voice—a miracle—

For a few minutes, I feel warmer—I think they are minutes for I have lost all count of time. Then, as in choral crescendo the winds wrap roaring round the plane, the fear within me starts again to snarl—"HANNA-A-A—", it hesitates, then, in one savage leap, it pounces—and the jaws of terror close.

Quite suddenly, it has become lighter and now it is getting lighter still. I raise my eyes,—no sky to be seen! But what I do see is earth, dark brown earth,—above me! I see it when I look up—and when I look down, clouds, white streamers, stringing along in line. Now I know that I am flying upside-down.

Mechanically, I seize the control column, and the situation is reversed. Under me, the earth, with far away and just discernible, the snow-white peaks of the Riesengebirge;

above me, the white clouds, breaking up, and higher yet, drawing slowly away, the towering pillar of the storm-cloud. As it goes, it spews out a multitude of greying wisps as, a few minutes ago, it spewed me out, head-first, into space.

Once more in the blessed light, I am feeling no more terror or pain as slowly, softly, I glide on the silver-grey wings of my bird, thought-free and free of all feeling save that of profound gratitude.

We are floating down towards the glittering white ridge of the Riesengebirge. I can already distinguish the mountain huts and the little black dots of the skiers, turning homeward at close of day. Here, on the Schneekoppe, I will make my landing, where there are people to help.

It was already late afternoon when I touched down beside the hotel-restaurant on the Schneekoppe, the daylight was beginning to fade and the skiers had all vanished from the slopes. So I was able, undisturbed, to make fast the glider, piling snow on the wing-tips to prevent the wind from carrying her away. As I did so, I saw how the wings had been holed in countless places by the hail stones.

My plane and I would somehow have to get back to Hirschberg that very evening and that meant I would have to telephone to Wolf Hirth so that he could fly over and drop me a starting rope.

Bedraggled and sopping wet, I went into the hotel, encountering many suspicious glances as I waited for my call to come through. Around me, all was gusty fellowship and good cheer, the guests chattering and laughing in an atmosphere blue with tobacco smoke and laced with the aroma of freshly ground coffee. But of these surroundings I was barely conscious, hearing only the ebb and flow of laughter and voices and, somewhere in the background, a zither's fragmentary sound. If only my call would come through!

And then someone saw the "Grunau-Baby." Immediately, there was a wild stampede among the guests, all thronging to the windows to see the Incomprehensible with their own eyes. I went with them, as if it were no concern of mine. I found a fat, middle-aged man beside me, almost sweating with emotion.

"Fräulein," he stammered, "I tell you, it has descended just—just like the Incarnate One. It certainly wa-wasn't standing there five minutes ago . . ."

He could get no further, for at that moment his wife tugged him by the coat and drew him away. He ought not to have gone talking to such a raggamuffin, I heard her say, as she marched him angrily towards the door . . .

The rest was lost, for I was now called to the telephone.

"Hanna!" Wolf Hirth shouted, "Where in God's name are you?" I hardly had time to answer before a torrent of words roared into my ear, leaving me completely numbed and thinking only that, somehow, I must be in the storm-cloud again. Seconds later, I realised what he had been saying. The Schneekoppe lay in the Neutral Zone adjoining the Czechoslovak frontier and in landing an aircraft there without permission, I had committed an offence which would probably entail the withdrawal of my flying permit.

I put down the receiver in utter despair. Never more certainly that at this moment, I knew, as every real flier must, that flying was my whole life—I could not live without it.

Once they had got over the shock of my appearance, they did everything they could at the hotel to cheer me up. In desperation, they even put on a special film-show for me. But it was no good. No good, until I was told that Wolf Hirth wanted me on the telephone again urgently. This time he spoke very briefly. He told me to get ready for the take-off, collect as many people as possible in a great circle outside the hotel and wait till he flew over and dropped the starting-rope, in about half-an-hour.

In a flash, my gloom dispersed and I was filled with jubilation. The hotel guests willingly did I as asked them and spread out, marking a great circle on the snow-field. Though it was now almost dark and the cold was intense, no one complained and all waited tensely expectant, straining to catch the first faint throb of an aircraft. Within the half-hour, Wolf Hirth flew over, dropped a package in the circle we had marked out for him, roared up over our heads and receded once more into the night.

Now I had the starting-rope and a flag with a message attached telling me how to take off and what arrangements were being made for the landing. They were going to collect as many cars as possible in the valley below and flood-light a landing-ground for me.

From among the hotel guests I now picked two teams, each of ten men, to stand at each end of the starting-rope. They were told what they had to do and first we practiced without connecting the glider, so that they could get accustomed to the various words of command and learn to run with the rope at speed towards the edge of the precipice without giving way to the impulse to slow up. Otherwise, the take-off would, quite literally, be a flop. When all were proficient, I climbed into the glider, buckled my parachute harness and gave the signal to go.

Meanwhile, Wolf Hirth, with Edmund Schneider, the designer of the "Grunau-Baby," had been circling above us in his plane, like an anxious clucking hen whose chick has gone exploring on its own—and after dark, at that!

Never in my life have I had a better take-off. The teams put so much energy into their task that the glider soared up with terrific impetus and the next moment was hovering over the mountain side. Below me, I could just make out the dim, receding shapes of woods and fields and, here and there, a village, beckoning with a cluster of lights, while overhead there stretched a velvet, darkening expanse, pricked through, one by one, by the glittering sword-points of the stars.

Above me, flew Wolf Hirth, his small machine showing black against the sky. He was showing the identification lights required by international convention, green on the starboard wing, red on the port, one white light at the nose and another at the tail.

I had hoped to be able to reach the airfield at Hirschberg,

as I soon found that it would be quite impossible to pick out
the small illuminated patch of landing-ground from among
the lights of the villages in the valley. But first, I had to fly
over a medium-sized hill and, the glider fast losing height, I
decided the safer course would be to land as soon as I could.

I search round anxiously and catch sight of what looks like
an open field. But in the gathering darkness, I cannot be sure.
It would be easy not to see small clumps of trees, even a
house. But I will try it. I put the glider down right at the
edge of the field, she bumps a little, then slithers to a stop.
At last, I am on brown earth again.

For a while, I feel no desire to move and sit in drowsy
bliss, the tension slowly ebbing from my mind. Wolf Hirth is
happy, too; I can see and hear it as, having thus far hovered
protectively overhead, he suddenly roars up his engine, dips
his wings, then curves away and, quickly gaining speed,
flies off—to arrange, I hope, for a car to fetch me.

I listen to his engine as it roars, hums, throbs and finally
sinks away in the distance.

And now there is silence, everywhere. Earth and sky seem
wrapped in sleep. My glider-bird slumbers, too, gleaming
softly against the stars. Beautiful bird, that out-flew the four
winds, braved the tempest, shot heavenward, searching out
the sky,—soaring higher, as I am soon to learn, than any
glider-plane has ever flown before.

## 6. I Become a Gliding Instructor

A FEW WEEKS after my flight in the storm-cloud, Wolf Hirth was appointed to be Head of the new Gliding School at the Hornberg, near Gmünd in Swabia. He wanted to take me with him as an instructor and obtained, as I was eager to go, my parents' permission for me to miss the following term at school.

In due course, we moved to the Hornberg and I was faced with the prospect of having to start, within a few days, to teach grown men to be glider pilots and prepare them for their "C" Tests.

Only now did I fully realise the difficulty of the task which I had undertaken. Already during my own training in Grunau, I had learnt that men, while treating their own desire to become glider pilots as natural and normal, tend to look on any girl who professes a similar inclination as the victim of a mere foolish whim and though my seriousness of purpose and my natural capacity for this sport had perhaps taught them to think differently, I realised that, whatever the sphere, men do not like being taught by a girl and particularly in gliding, which has always had the reputation of being an especially virile pastime.

With this in mind, I attempted from the start to avoid, with my trainees, the usual relationship of master and pupil and I turned the lessons into a sort of discussion group, based on joint effort. This was fairly easy in the practical classes. If, for example, a glider had come back from the workshop after repair, I would say that Wolf Hirth had made me personally responsible for testing its airworthiness and that I, therefore, had to fly it before any of my pupils. Thus, by watching me handle the plane, they would learn some of the technique of gliding. Or I would ask a pupil to make a practice flight and point out to the others, while he was in the

air, what was right or wrong in his handling of the plane.
When he landed, I would not wait, as instructors usually did,
at the top of the slope, while my pupils ran down and hauled
the plane up, but acted throughout as if I were one of them.

In theoretical instruction—held indoors in the evenings—
the discussion-group method was harder to apply. But I was
determined to avoid the role of pedagogue and eventually I
found a way. I would ask my pupils to choose a subject on
which they would like me to talk. They usually chose my
gliding experiences. I would then use the incidents in my
story as a means of introducing the theoretical points which
I wanted them to learn. Gliding in a storm-cloud, for
example, I used as a lead-in to a lecture on the use of
instruments.

In this way, I managed to lull my pupils into forgetting
that they were being instructed in the manly sport of gliding
by a mere school-girl and, as a result, a noticeably enthusiastic and happy atmosphere prevailed throughout the course.

Wolf Hirth was at first dubious of the success of my
methods and was greatly relieved to find that, by the end of
the course, all my pupils were well up to standard. But I
myself was not far from the point of total exhaustion.

A tragic incident marred the end of this chapter in my
flying career. On the last day of the course, there was still
one pupil who had not yet qualified for his "C" Certificate.
He and I remained behind, alone, while the others, having
all passed the day before, set out for Stuttgart-Böblingen to
have their first experience of towed flight.

Before this last pupil took off for his test, I went with him
carefully, point by point, through every aspect of his flight.
He had done well in his "A" and "B" Tests and, seeming
now perfectly at ease and sure of himself, would, I had no
doubt, pass this last one quite easily.

He took off in his glider normally and then, for a whole
two and a half minutes, flew exactly as the book, without a
fault. Now he had only to fly one turn, circle wide and land.
He turned—rather steep but quite well—and then,—
plunged in one straight swift dive to earth.

I had never heard before what sound a plane makes when it crashes and at first I could not move. Then I ran down the hillside towards the wreckage, knowing, as I ran, that my pupil was already dead.

It fell to me to break the news to his mother, who lived in a nearby village.

I will never forget how I walked to her cottage through the fields, alone, how the poor, old woman saw me coming and called to me before I could speak:

"*Ach, Fräuleinchen—ich weiss schon. Mein Sohn! Mein Sohn ist nicht mehr.*"

—how could she know?

Then, as she took me weeping in her arms, she told me that, before he left his home that morning her son had spoken of the crash. She had tried to hold him back, but he had comforted her, saying:

"No, mother, please—I'll manage it. I wish to go . . ." Those were the words, when, for the last time, she had heard the sound of his voice.

Later that day, I made enquiries among the airfield personnel and learnt that he had told one of them about a dream he had dreamed the night before. ". . . then, suddenly, I am in a steep turn, I jab the rudder with my feet, I touch the elevator—and then, I——"

Premonition? Or was it rather that the man had been basically unsure of himself and his dream was no more than an expression of this uncertainty? Perhaps the tragedy would not have happened if, by pure chance, he had not made exactly the same steep turn in his test as he had dreamed of the night before. Then, perhaps, as he turned, he suddenly recalled the dream and, his confidence failing him, moved the wrong controls, putting the plane into a vertical dive . . .

However that might be, my pupil was dead and many months were to pass before the horror of it had lifted from my mind.

# 7. The Rhön Soaring Contests

THE STORY of the Rhön Soaring Contests is closely connected with the history of the years following the First World War.

Under the Treaty of Versailles, Germany had been forbidden to possess engine-propelled aircraft, but, nevertheless, the longing to fly remained, a longing akin to homesickness, which, when it remains for too long unsatisfied, can make men physically ill.

Oskar Ursinus was one of many who were stricken by it. He went to the Rhön and sat on the hillside, watching the clouds sail past him against the pure blue sky. If only he could be up there! He saw the falcons and the buzzards, hovering on the wind against the hillside. If only he could fly like those birds, as Otto Lilienthal had done, without engine, with the aid only of Nature, by using the winds and the slopes of the hills!

At the Wasserkuppe there was wind in plenty, for it rises 1,300 feet above the plain and the air currents, sweeping against its sides, are deflected violently upwards. Indeed, the Wasserkuppe seemed to Oskar Ursinus ideal for his purpose and there, in the summer of 1920, he and his friends—airmen from the First World War, scientists, technicians and young people from all walks of life—attempted engineless flight, repairing old planes, improvising, building gliders that seem to us now like relics from a prehistoric age. The first flights lasted for a matter of seconds, somewhat like our modern "A" Tests, and the longest flight that summer was only two minutes and twenty-two seconds, covering a distance of two-thousand-and-forty-eight yards, but it was a triumph, nevertheless.

From that time on, summer after summer, young glider pilots came to the Wasserkuppe to try out their machines and their skill, learning as they did so more and more about the forces of Nature and how to exploit them. Many there were who sacrificed time and money, not a few, their career, and some, their lives. But gradually, out of their efforts, grew the recognition in Germany and the world that gliding had emerged from the realm of dream and theory to become a practical reality.

When I went to the Wasserkuppe for the first time in the Summer of 1933, the Rhön Contests, as they were called, were already a recognised annual event and were attended by all who possessed or aspired to a name in German gliding.

As for me, my efforts in the Contests were ill-starred from the very beginning. I had come straight from the funeral of my former pupil and was still overshadowed by his tragic end. For the Contests, I had chosen to fly a Grunau-Baby training glider, though this type would stand little chance against some high-performance sailplanes that had been entered. The terrain was unknown to me and the weather conditions proved to be unfavourable to my type of machine.

Moreover, labouring as I was under the stress of recent events, with my mind not free to give of its best, I could not help but look on it as an added burden that the other competitors as well as the members of my own launching team, whom I had recruited from my former pupils at the Hornberg, should treat me as a kind of Wizard of the Air, from whom prodigies might confidently be expected.

They were soon to be disillusioned. Immediately after my first take-off, I found myself rapidly losing height and for lack of an up-current had to land in the valley. And there I had, perforce, to sit, while the other competitors, with their better machines and greater experience, continued to sail on above me.

My launching team came running down the slope, disappointment clearly written in their faces. How proud they had been of their diminutive pilot!

"That's all right, it doesn't matter, doesn't matter a bit!" I managed to tell them. "We'll dismantle her quickly and get her up to the top again. I'll soon get the feel of it."

So we got her up to the top again, again I took off and again I flopped, and so it continued, like some nightmare routine, throughout the remainder of that day. Each time my team had to come pelting down the slope to retrieve me, their disappointment waxed and my courage waned,—did it always have to be their pilot who was sitting in the ditch?

Misfortune never lacks for scoffers and my plight aroused much mirth among the onlookers. I suppose if I had been in their place, I would have found it funny, too. As it was, their laughter made me feel resentful and I could not restrain the tears that started to my eyes. To my team, however, I managed to keep up an appearance of spirited unconcern.

Day after day, while the Contests lasted, my fate was the same, but I did not give up and each time I flopped, I took off afresh in the hope of better luck.

On the final day, there was a farewell celebration and prize-giving. Among the firms who regularly donated prizes, a manufacturer of kitchen equipment had presented a meat mincer and a set of kitchen scales. These objects proved somewhat of an embarrassment to the awarding committee until someone hit on the idea of presenting them to me, as a "booby"-prize and perhaps also as a warning to any other forward little girls who might set their hearts on flying!

The award provoked uproarious laughter, but a more pleasant kind of prize was yet to come.

At the end of the festivities, Professor Georgii, already at that time known as "the Professor of Soaring," or "the Professoarer," asked me whether I would be willing to join an expedition to study thermal conditions in South America.

Why, it may be asked, after my lack of success in the Contests, did he pick on me rather than on one of the many more experienced and skilful pilots who had taken part? Strange as it may sound, it was my very failure that had decided him to do so. In his address to the prize-winners, both he and Oskar Ursinus, the founder of the Contests, had referred to my persistent refusal to give up in the face of bad luck, pointing the moral that in soaring it is not success but the spirit which counts.

My efforts, at any rate, had decided the Professor to invite me and without hesitation I accepted, so long as my parents permission could be obtained. The fact that I was required to contribute 3,000 Marks to the expenses of the expedition and that I had not the faintest idea where they were to come from, seemed to me, young as I was, to be only a minor detail.

## 8. Stunt Flying for the Films

A MONG THE many letters which I received after my altitude record in the storm-cloud was one from the film company, Ufa, asking me to take part as a "double" in a film about gliding. At that time, I had put the letter on one side, but now I remembered it, wondering whether here, perhaps, was an opportunity to acquire the money which I needed for the South America expedition.

I wrote to Ufa accepting their invitation and was asked to go and see them. After we had discussed and agreed on general terms, I stipulated as a fee the sum I was required to contribute to the expedition,—three thousand Marks.

I spoke the words and then held my breath. Probably they would think I was mad, or else they would take it for a joke and break out in peals of laughter. But I had no choice; three thousand Marks, and nothing less, I had to have before I could go to South America.

To my boundless amazement, they agreed without demur —like they do on the films!

The film was called "Rivals of the Air" and was shot at the Rhön in Thuringia and in East Prussia, on the narrow tongue of land South of Memel, on the shores of the Baltic.

The story concerned a young gliding enthusiast who persuades a girl friend to go on a training course with him.

As the best pupil on the course, he is then allowed as a reward to take part in the Soaring Contests at the Wasserkuppe; but not, however, the girl, who has proved totally unsuited to flying. But, being a small and energetic person, on that subject she has some ideas of her own . . .

The Contests begin. The young man takes off, so does his former flying instructor and many others. Meanwhile, the girl stands below, watching the beautiful silver birds go soaring high into the sky, and as she does so, she makes a decision. She goes to the hangar, where she finds a training glider that no one is using. With the help of some spectators she fetches it out, then takes off in pursuit of the other competitors. Soon she has reached the same height as they.

This manoeuvre has been noticed by only one person, the flying instructor, and now he notices something else—coming up from the West and drawing closer and closer is a great wall of thunder cloud; alone, the girl will never survive it . . .

So now, as he secretly loves her, the instructor resolves on the greatest sacrifice that a glider pilot can make: he throws away his chance of winning the Contest in order to lead the girl into the down-wind and show her the best place to make her landing. Of course, she bungles it and instead of coming down on to a meadow, flops straight into a lake, whence she emerges to wade, dripping, to the shore. There the instructor awaits her. At first, he is harsh and reproachful, but then—so that all may end happily—he folds her, still dripping, in his arms . . .

In this story, my role was to double for the girl in the flying sequences; as soon as there was dialogue, the actors took over. And what a wonderful part it was,—crashes galore! Where else would I have had such a chance?

The crash into the lake was not easy, for the "lake" turned out to be no more than a large-sized pool and the "pancake" landing had to be timed with absolute precision. However, all went well and I landed plumb in the middle of the water, giving vent, in joy at my success, to a loud "yippee!"

I had clean forgotten that the cameras were recording sound as well as vision and that, instead of the "cry of despair" which the story required, the girl would now be heard to give a yell of triumph!

And there was another point which emerged when we saw the rushes. The landing had succeeded so well that anyone acquainted with gliding would see immediately that no beginner could possibly have made it. So the sequence had to be shot all over again. This time, another pilot performed the crash, owing to contractual complications which would be of no interest here.

While we were on location on the Baltic, I spent all my spare time in flying. The beaches and sand dunes in this part of East Prussia are ideal for glider take-offs and in that particular part, the wind conditions were favourable, too. For a glider pilot, there can hardly be a more lovely experience than flying over those silent and magical vistas of shore, sea and sand. Each time I took off, I flew for as long as the wind would carry me, hovering, oblivious of time, over blue sea and yellow dunes beneath August and September skies.

On one occasion, I flew for nine hours and, on the following day, for eleven hours and twenty minutes, setting up two new World Endurance Records for Women. They were not internationally registered, as I had not intended to achieve them and therefore had not flown under the prescribed conditions.

But as for me, that question did not worry me, for I had only one desire—to fly as a bird flies, unfettered and wholly free.

## 9. Soaring in Brazil and the Argentine

ON 3rd JANUARY, 1934, the "Monte Pascoal" stood out from Hamburg for South America. There were larger ships and ships that were more luxurious, ships that travelled faster and ships that could boast of carrying more distinguished passengers, but to me, the "Monte Pascoal" and everything about her was unsurpassably magnificent and exciting. I had read about sea voyages but never been on one and as the ship slid slowly from her berth to the gay accompaniment of *"Muss i denn muss' i denn zum Städtele hinaus"* from the ship's band and I stood waving to my parents and friends from the rail, I looked forward to enjoying every moment of this, my first journey to foreign lands.

I was twenty-one and for that reason, perhaps, each smallest detail of the journey burnt itself in on my mind: the meals to which we had to accustom ourselves, so vast and so varied that the menus seemed almost endless, the company of people from other lands and continents, whose lives and background were so different from our own and, most intriguing of all, the ship with all its secrets. Here, the fact that I was the only girl in a party of men and that I was so small proved an unexpected advantage, for it assured me the Captain's benevolence and he made me his "smallest sailor," or "Moses," as he was known in this ship. As such I was given the freedom of the ship and could climb anywhere I liked, even up the masts.

Most of my time on board I spent in the company of the other members of the expedition, of which the leader was Professor Georgii, the "Professor of Soaring," meteorologist and President of the International Study Commission for Motorless Flight. Each day, under his supervision, we took various readings—radiation, wind-speed, height of the cloud-base, and others—thereby adding much to our theoretical knowledge of soaring.

The members of the expedition were all well-known glider pilots: Wolf Hirth with his sailplane "Moatzagotl," a unique design, Peter Riedel and the "Fafnir," Heini Dittmar with his "Condor," myself, with a "Grunau-Baby," and our faithful fitter and aircraft rigger, Miehm.

We soon became known to the other passengers as a group, but lacking at first any precise knowledge about us, they soon began to make conjectures. To some, we were a circus troupe, to others, a sailing club, while to the remainder we were either a bunch of raw, untutored flying enthusiasts or else the authentic wizards-of-the-air!

Throughout the voyage, I seemed to meet the charm of novelty at every turn, setting sail from Hamburg, for example: the night, the lights, the water, the driving ice floes which broke up on the bow with a sharp tinkle like a toast from a thousand glasses. Or in the North Sea, the heavy ground swell and the thick blanket of fog that suddenly descended, coming between the hand and the eyes, while the ship began to creep forward through the night, the siren sounding weirdly on a note of primitive fear—outside, the dark and the cold; within, warmth and reassurance and the heart of the ship beating powerfully against the surge and fall of the swell.

When we had passed through the Bay of Biscay, the swell subsided and the sky turned to cloudless blue, the weather becoming warmer and the nights, wonderfully mild. Slowly we accustomed ourselves to spending our days in idleness. We passed within some dozen miles of the Spanish coast, seeing in the distance tall, lonely looking cliffs, surmounted by the single white dots of houses. Then I saw the first dolphins, causing amusement by taking them for flying fish.

Having past Lisbon and Casablanca, we anchored, on the evening of the seventh day of our voyage, in the harbour of Las Palmas, the lights of the town shining to us from across the water, while a sickle moon glowed down, a golden-red, from a clear and starless sky. And suddenly, almost without transition, night turned into day and I saw bare, yellow cliffs (magnificent for gliding!) and, at their foot, with its flat roofs and occasional domes, the glittering white town.

As soon as we dropped anchor that evening, there began a pantomime, familiar to all acquainted with the East, but to me, completely new.

A swarm of little boats and canoes came scudding round the ship like water-flies, full of niggers, half-castes and, here and there, those tall and dignified figures, royal even in their rags, who one could see were of pure Spanish extraction. In a moment, they were all over the ship, some of them, dark and sinister looking, sending an involuntary shudder down the spine. They spread out their wares on the deck— bangles and baubles, kimonos, rugs, fruits—anything, so long as it was brightly coloured.

Passengers were allowed to land, but before going ashore my friends and I visited a German aircraft mother-ship that was lying in the harbour. After that, there was little time left for the town itself, though I saw enough to appreciate the, to me, utterly strange and intriguing atmosphere of the South. On the roadways of sand, the donkey carts went bumping over the deep holes, the street traders sat surrounded by silent groups of men, the women passed to and fro shrouded almost to the eyes in black, the children gambolled about, while in the background stretched a mournful waste of sand and dilapidated masonry. Unfortunately, there was no time for us to visit the more attractive quarters of the town.

As we weighed anchor, half-naked black boys, supple as fish, dived for coins which we threw them from the rail, while, over-topping all, the negro traders abjured us in frenzied tones to buy up their entire stock of wares.

Then, once more, we were at sea—glittering sun, swarms of flying fishes, the Equator and "Father Neptune" and, at last, Rio de Janeiro, that rightly claims to be the most beautiful harbour-city in the world. To the traveller from the Northern Hemisphere, the approach to Rio is like entering a paradise.

Our hotel lay high up on a mountain that towered steeply over the sea. Before it lay a lovely old monastery garden, with trees of which no one could tell me the name, with palms and hedges full of blossom, some a fiery red and others of clearer and more delicate hues.

I received my first surprise when I opened my suitcases. They were swarming with ants, which bit me terribly. I spent half the night getting rid of them, cleaning them out of each piece of clothing separately. After that experience, no insects that South America could offer were able to disconcert me!

The city was, indeed, as we had been told, both beautiful and elegant. For my friends, the only unpleasant aspect was that white men never permitted themselves to go about in shirt sleeves. But we all found that we had to revise our ideas about time. We had already had a foretaste of Spanish dilatoriness during the formalities of landing. Though bureaucracy in Germany often placed a severe strain on its citizens' nerves, it was something more than red-tape that we encountered here—it was the cult of "tomorrow," "mañana," the most important and overworked word in the Spanish language.

On disembarking, we had taken it in good part, with impatience, admittedly, but with respect for the customs of strange lands. But it was another matter when our gliders remained for a whole three weeks under seal at the Customs, while Government Departments argued over questions of competency. Each time we were told that they would be released "tomorrow," we became more and more anxious and we only really began to feel at ease in South America when we knew that they had been loaded on to the transporters and were on their way to the airfield.

Meanwhile, we were never idle, press conferences alternating with receptions and big meals, interlaced with solemn speeches amid settings of the utmost floral magnificence. Particularly assiduous were the journalists, for news of our expedition had quickly spread and, gliding being then in its infancy in Brazil, everyone was eagerly awaiting the moment when our planes would take to the air. The presence of a girl in the expedition naturally increased the interest and curiosity, especially in these southern climes.

At last, our silver birds made their appearance, the splendid "Fafnir," in which Grönhoff had achieved his great successes, the "Condor," the "Moatzagotl" and my modest "Grunau-Baby." The object of our expedition was to study up-wind conditions in South America—a private affair, in no way intended as a good-will tour. But we had no need to woo our hosts, for they took us immediately to their hearts in a manner so spontaneous and overwhelming as we would never have thought possible.

The interest in our activities was enormous. Each day hundreds and thousands of the city's inhabitants trekked out to the airfield to watch us fly. What interested them most were the aerobatics and while my colleagues performed them only rarely, to my regret, I had to fly them almost every day. I would much have preferred to have been taking part in cross-country flights, as would anyone whose heart is in gliding. But on an expedition, discipline is everything and so, uncomplaining, I flew my loops and turns to the delight and enthusiasm of the men and women, the officers and the shoals upon shoals of school children who came out every day to watch.

After about four weeks, we transferred from Rio to San Paulo and here, the same experiences were repeated—receptions, interviews with the Press and the enthusiasm of the population.

But San Paulo brought also the unexpected, in the shape of a narrow shave with disaster.

I had little experience of "thermal" flying, that is, flights in the type of up-wind which is caused by the warmth of the ground being transferred to the air above it. I was therefore also ignorant of the fact that, in certain conditions, a kind of "thermal air bubble" can come up from the ground, to rise above a glider pilot at the very moment when he is trying to make use of it.

That was to be my experience one Sunday morning in San

Paulo. It was a wonderful day, with the cloud base at about 6,500 feet, and when we had foregathered on the airfield on the outskirts of the city, we cast lots to decide the order in which we should be towed up in our gliders. I was the last and when it finally came to my turn, Peter Riedel and Heini Dittmar were already far above, hovering like tiny specks beneath the clouds.

The wind was in such a position that we had to take off directly towards the town. Still quite low over the streets and still on tow, my machine began to quiver, then lift gently upwards, straining against the tow-rope. Thinking I would be able to climb much faster on my own—perhaps at about 15 feet per second—than the engined machine would be able to tow me up, I decided to cast off. Having done so, hardly had I circled once than I began to lose height. So, little knowing that the "thermal bubble" had already passed over my head and all about me was nothing but down-wind, I started to search round in the hope of finding the up-wind again.

Below me, the great city spread out into the distance, with its roofs and towers, churches and chimneys and long, straight streets, crowded with traffic and pedestrians. Steadily this jig-saw of brick and humanity reared up towards me and I realised that in a few moments I would be forced to land. I looked round for a flat roof, but they all seemed either to have roof-gardens or to be surrounded with chimney stacks. I was already in desperation, my mind's eye seeing a terrible slaughter as I crashed into a street, when, in the distance, I saw what looked like an open field. Still steadily losing height, I made towards it, to find, as I approached, that it was a football ground, fringed on all sides with a dense throng of spectators watching a game in full progress. The shock almost took my breath away, for it was by no means certain that I could clear the crowd. Then I saw that I could just miss them and land on the ground, but— fresh terror!—along the side which I was approaching, there stretched a high tension cable: I would have to fly under it close over the spectators' heads.

Even then, the danger would not be over. The game was at its height and all eyes being concentrated on the players, my plane would probably not even be noticed as it glided noiselessly down. And if anyone did see it, he would assume that it was a motor aircraft that, having reached the crowd, would immediately roar up again over their heads.

And so it was—nobody dreamed of stopping the game. I tore open the window and, with all my strength, yelled one of the few Spanish words that I knew: *"Cuidado! Cuidado!"* "Beware! Beware!" For a few seconds, then, they did stop the game to look up at me, but no one seemed to be in any doubt that I would open up the engine and fly off again and not one of the thousands seemed to realise that he was in mortal danger, that I had got to land!

Finally, as I swooped clean through a goal-mouth, the truth dawned and, at the last second, the footballers flung themselves to the ground.

By good luck, no one was injured or even touched. I stood up, my machine intact and on level ground, and, expelling a great sigh of relief, started to unbuckle my parachute harness, then turned, to see—the most terrifying sight of all!

A great mob of people, thousands strong, had broken through the barriers and was flooding towards me across the field.

I imagined the wings of my plane cracking and breaking under this tide, what remained being then trampled to pieces underfoot. In desperation, I climbed on to a wing so that all could see me and waved to them to hold back. But my action merely whetted their curiosity further. They found it quite enchanting and, in their delight and enthusiasm, took off their hats, waved their thanks and blew kisses to me. Meanwhile, the human tide was approaching, each man pressing through in an effort to be the first to touch the plane.

At last, through a sea of faces, I caught sight of uniforms. The military had arrived, but too few of them to be effective. Then a German came to my aid and called the mounted police. Making straight towards me, they forced a passage ruthlessly through the throng, anyone who failed to make way being trampled beneath the horses' hooves. Soon a cry went up for first aid and ambulances arrived to carry away the injured. Then, on their prancing, mettlesome horses, the police formed a cordon round me, galloping continually in a circle like a roundabout at a fair, until I became giddy at the sight of them and had to close my eyes.

Meanwhile, the pilot of my towing-plane had been circling overhead, filled with concern, never imagining that I had cast off of my own free will so low over the city and assuming that the tow-rope must have broken in two. But now, seeing that all was well, he flew back to the airfield to inform the others and arrange for a car to fetch me and a transporter to collect the glider. Professor Georgii and my other friends had also been anxiously watching my experiment, for the success of the expedition would naturally have been endangered if an accident had befallen any of its members.

As it was, the incident turned out to be the most successful prelude to our stay in San Paulo. The newspapers were full of it, the population delighted, for, being unfamiliar with gliding, they none of them seemed to guess the danger to which the football crowd had been exposed and continued to think of the incident as—the Strange and Marvellous Case of the Girl who Fell from the Sky!

From San Paulo, which lies about 280 miles inland from Rio de Janeiro, we had good opportunities of carrying out long-distance soaring flights.

Though Brazil, with its vast, unpopulated plains and virgin forest was full of dangers for glider pilots who, like us, did not know the country, we soon found ourselves undertaking ambitious flights, thanks, largely, to the black vultures, or "Urubus," as the natives called them.

These birds feed on carrion and in South America act as a kind of sanitary service. As soon as they see flesh that is beginning to decompose, they descend in dense, black swarms and consume it with unbelievable speed. About as large as a goose, they are revoltingly ugly, with their grey plumage and bare, featherless heads, but they are wonderful

thermal gliders. We always searched round for them as soon
as we took off, for we quickly discovered that wherever they
were to be seen, hovering with motionless wings in the air,
we too would be able to soar in our gliders.

The "Urubus" were easy to find, as they almost always
appeared in groups of several hundred birds together. They
never flew off at our approach or even bothered to make way
for the plane and they often came so close to the cabin that
one involuntarily drew one's head in. So we would circle up,
surrounded by the vultures, as high as the thermals would
carry us, then, gliding down, head in our chosen direction,
all the while keeping a look-out for the next cluster of birds
so that we could work out way up again. In this manner, we
found it possible to fly over wide stretches of lonely plain and
forest, which we would never have been able to do without
the aid of our reliable "pilots."

Finding the Urubus so helpful, we conceived the idea of
taking some back with us to Germany. What records would
we not be able to achieve in the Rhön Soaring Contests, for
example, if each of us had our own private Urubu! So at
Bahia, on the return voyage, we took four of them on board,
placing them in a large, open-air cage on the top deck and
supplying them daily with large quantities of meat and fish.

So as to acclimatize them as gently as possible, we took
them, on our arrival in Germany, to Darmstadt, which is
well known for its mildness. Darmstadt was also the home of
the Institute for Glider Research, of which Professor Georgii
was the Director. The beasts were given a beautiful big cage
and we continued to feed them with devotion and zeal,
though, in the light of its effects, I would not presume to
claim that the diet which we selected for them was by any
means the most suitable for our purpose. We were bold
enough to hope that, when we opened the door of their cage,
they would take off for a short demonstration of soaring
flight and then return of their own accord to their dining-
room, but when, after some three weeks, we finally did so,
the birds with one accord refused to budge.

In vain we chivvied, enticed and cajoled, the Urubus

stayed exactly where they were, hardly bothering, even, to take a single step, let alone to spread their wings. So we had no alternative but to take long poles and positively drive them out of their cage. But even then, they refused to fly, clambering, instead, like monkeys—only with considerably less skill—up the trunks of some nearby trees, there to settle themselves contentedly in the branches. We were powerless. We thought of taking them up in a plane, but then decided it would be useless, as they would probably crash to the ground. Apart from that, they pecked so fiercely at anything within reach, that in our small sports planes, which were the only ones available to us, we would have been exposing ourselves to considerable danger.

However, in due course one of the Urubus decided to become independent and walked to Heidelberg, where it was seen in the streets. It was even said to have been seen crossing the Rhine on the ferry, but the source of this information was unreliable and I cannot say if that detail is correct.

We gave the other three birds to the Frankfurt Zoo, where we all hoped they would begin a new and more useful chapter in their lives.

I have already mentioned that the real object of our expedition to South America was to study the up-winds there and the first thing that we noticed about them was their extraordinary force compared with the up-winds at home, due to the intensity of the heat. Moreover they began to form quite early in the morning. In coastal areas, however—for example, at Rio de Janeiro in Brazil and Buenos Aires in the Argentine—the up-winds were dissipated during the course of the forenoon by the breezes which began to blow in from the sea and thereafter only down-winds were to be found.

In the afternoons, therefore, we usually confined ourselves to flying demonstration flights, large crowds coming every day to the airfield to watch us. Thanks to these free entertainments, we received innumerable invitations from flying enthusiasts all over Brazil, while amateur gliding clubs began to spring up everywhere.

One invitation came from the fair-sized German colony of Curitiba, the capital of Parana, one of the Provinces of Brazil, and just before our departure for the Argentine, I spent an enjoyable day there as the official representative of our expedition. The enthusiasm of my compatriots was great and they welcomed me with everything that was possible to cram into the few hours I was with them: flowers, speeches, gifts, and public receptions. In the afternoon, I went on foot with the members of the newly formed gliding club to inspect the sites which they had selected for their future activities.

In the Argentine, no less than in Brazil, we received a cordial welcome. Again there were demonstration flights and, above all, aerobatics, during which Wolf Hirth performed seventy-six successive loops, so setting up a new world record.

With the limitless flat expanses of the pampas, the Argentine is the ideal country for long-distance soaring and here I carried out my first flight of this kind, for which I received the Silver Soaring Medal, the first woman to do so.

During the flight, I had flown for two-and-a-half to three hours inland from Buenos Aires over a typical Argentine landscape—not a house, not a road, not a living soul, nothing but endless vistas of pampas covered with grazing herds. At last, I was caught in a down-wind and had to land. I touched down beside one of the rare villages, seemingly deserted and lifeless in the broiling heat.

As I got out of the plane, I was confronted with six savage-looking horses. Feeling vaguely that South American horses might differ temperamentally from those to which I was accustomed, I decided it would be wiser not to move. Herds of cattle, I had been told, had been known to attack suddenly any stranger who ventured too close to them. And so, the horses, which surprisingly remained at a respectable distance, stood staring at me and I stared back at the horses.

Determined not to be the first to move, I waited for something to happen: perhaps the horses would move away, or someone see me from the village. After a time—how long, I do not know—an aged Ford came rattling up, from which two friendly Argentinians emerged. I made myself understood as best I could in Spanish, whereupon one of them escorted me to the village, while his companion stayed behind to guard the plane. My appearance provoked wild excitement among the villagers, starved, as they were, of the unexpected, and the "Gloria Allemana," as they called me, hardly knew where to turn for the hospitality which was pressed upon her.

Shortly afterwards, Heini Dittmar, who had been towed up from the airfield at Buenos Aires at about the same time as myself, had to land in his glider, also, thank God, not far from the same village.

And then a further visitor appeared—Wolf Hirth! He had landed in his "Moatzagotl" about ten miles away, to find himself alone on a vast expanse surrounded by herds of cattle and horses. After a time, three wild-looking men had appeared and offered to help him. To their minds, the simplest solution was to round up one of the horses so that he could ride on it to the village. Wolf Hirth explained that he had an artificial limb and so could not make use of their friendly offer and they then produced, seemingly from nowhere, a cart, in which, groaning and lurching through mud, mire and rubble, they drove him in state to the village.

On that same day, Peter Riedel had been luckier than we, gliding in his "Fafnir" for a distance of ninety-three miles— in those days, a considerable feat.

When, on 13th April, we embarked for the voyage home, we took with us a rich harvest in flying achievement. Peter Riedel had set up a new record for long-distance soaring, Heini Dittmar, a world altitude record and I had received the Silver Soaring Medal, the first woman and the twenty-fifth among the world's glider pilots to do so.

But more important than our success in flying or than the scientific results of the expedition were the good relations which we had established with our South American hosts. We had built a bridge of friendship, of mutual respect and understanding, and that was the most valuable achievement of all.

## 10.  The German Institute for Glider Research

FROM THE deck of "The General San Martin," we watched as Buenos Aires—and South America—dwindled and dissolved out of our sight, our friends waving from the shore, at first clearly recognisable still, then merging into the dark streak of the mole at the harbour mouth, then the narrow harbour itself falling away to silence astern. Our visit was over.

But when, still full of our experiences, we sat talking together, while the ship sailed on across the open sea, each day seemed to come alive for us again, every flight and every cloud.

I stood with Professor Georgii at the ship's rail, summoning up picture upon picture of those unforgettable weeks, which had strengthened, if possible, yet further my love of flying. Now I knew it would burn in me always.

"But, Hanna," said Professor Georgii suddenly, breaking in on my thoughts, "we can't let you leave us now. From now on, you belong to us, in Darmstadt, at the Institute."

And so, accepting Professor Georgii's invitation, I became a member, in June, 1934, of the German Institute for Glider Research. The Institute had developed out of the old Rhön-Rossiten-Gesellschaft, founded in 1925 by a group of pioneers for the purpose of research into the possibilities of motorless flight. Research was at first carried out by the new Institute at the Wasserkuppe, but as towing planes were required, for example when investigating the characteristics of up-winds, and there was no adequate airfield for them there, the Institute was transferred in 1933 to Darmstadt-Griesheim.

There, under the Directorship of Professor Georgii, it developed and extended its activities, becoming of great importance for the future of German gliding. It was thanks to him that during the following years when aviation in all its forms became a part of everyday life in Germany, the Institute lost nothing of its standing as the only organisation of its kind in the country and hence the centre of glider research throughout the world.

The Institute was divided into several departments, each with its special tasks, the meteorological department, for example, and the gliding department for which I was later to become test-pilot. The latter was concerned with the development and construction of all types of sailplanes, trainers, high-performance planes, special-purpose planes, etc. There was also a department that specialised in aircraft instruments, yet another held training courses for flight engineers. Further departments and sections of the Institute were devoted to research in technical aeronautics, including wind-tunnel tests and experiments with radio-controlled aircraft.

I belonged to the Institute for eleven years, until May, 1945. When I first joined, it was still in its infancy and the work had not yet become specialised in the departments I have mentioned. We pilots, therefore, had in those days no distinctly allotted tasks and we took on whatever was to hand. Together with Heini Dittmar, I was concerned mostly with meteorological flights, long-distance flights and altitude flights. Here I was in my element and I could hardly conceive a greater happiness than these tasks afforded.

During my first few weeks in Darmstadt, I succeeded, in off-duty hours, in setting up a new Women's World Record in long-distance soaring, covering a distance of over a hundred miles.

# Training Glider Pilots in Finland

IN UNDER three months, I was again asked to take part in an expedition, this time, to Finland. The Finnish Government had invited a group of German glider pilots to their country to hold demonstration flights and training courses with the object of stimulating interest in gliding among Finnish youth.

Our expedition was headed by Graf Ysenburg, among the members being Professor Rheindorf and, as pilots, Dr. Küttner from Breslau, Philipp from Berlin and Utech and myself from Darmstadt.

We reached Finland in September and, apart from the well-known features of the Finnish landscape—its spaciousness, its innumerable lakes, its dense, black forests—I was immediately struck by the intensity of the pure, bright colours and by the wonderful clarity of light and air. But the country as a whole seemed to dwell in loneliness, silent as though guarding a secret. The silence here seemed not merely absence of sound, but something positive, palpable almost. The endless country roads were silent, silent the narrow tracks that were the only link between lonely hamlets, strewn sparsely over the countryside. Now and again, in winter, would come the sound of a sleigh-bell, then once more a stillness would close over the land.

The Finns were like their country, taciturn, almost Oriental in their reserve, forming a strangely affecting contrast with the Western civilisation of their towns. They were also proud and honest and, above all, healthy.

The Finnish people owe their health, in the first place, to their natural and simple style of living. They allow light and air to get to their bodies and reserve to sport a place of honour in their national life. There is hardly a village, school or factory in Finland that does not possess the most

modern and generous facilities for sport. A further cause of
the astounding fitness of the Finns is that national institution,
the Sauna bath.

The Sauna bath is taken inside a wooden house consisting
of two rooms, in the first of which stands a stove, surfaced
with tiles specially made to transmit the heat. Close under
the rafters is a raised platform, or internal balcony, reached
by a ladder from inside the room. Here, the sweat-bath is
taken, while the air is filled with the unbelievably pleasant
and refreshing scent of young birch shoots which, after being
dried with their leaves for a year, are dipped in cold water
and held against the stove. These same birch rods are then
immersed again and used to switch the skin till the whole
body glows and tingles with a wonderful feeling of well-being.

Having remained in the heat on the balcony for some
minutes, the bather then descends, scrubs himself down with
a stiff brush, douses himself with buckets of water at varying
temperatures, then returns to the balcony for a further few
minutes.

This process is repeated two or three times and then—
almost all Sauna baths being built by the side of a lake—the
bather goes down into the second room and from there
plunges straight into the icy waters of the lake, swims a
couple of strokes and then comes out again. If the surface of
the lake is frozen over, he rolls, instead, in the snow.

Can it be wondered that, with these Sauna baths, the Finns
are a hardy and healthy people?

At every turn in Finland, we saw how the people lived in
the closest contact with Nature and, to our eyes, even the
humblest of those wooden homes, with their red and white
window frames, had a suggestion of spaciousness about it,
set, as it was, amid well-nigh limitless expanses of natural
scenery. Though the buildings in the towns are comparatively modern, they, too, lacked all sense of oppressive con-
finement, thanks to the wonderfully clean and unspoilt
countryside that lay at their very door.

Though the Finns are small in numbers, they have a

proud record of sporting achievement and we found that, like the South Americans, they took to gliding with an eager enthusiasm which showed itself not only in the large number of letters which we received during our visit and the even larger numbers that followed us home, but also in the warmth and appreciation with which speakers referred to our activities on a wide variety of official occasions.

So it was that, after our departure, a team of German technicians went over to teach the Finns how to construct training gliders and to help them set up the necessary workshops. Significant of the spirit in which the members of the Finnish Government approached the whole question of gliding, was their conviction that every village throughout the country should be encouraged to take it up, while the regulations which were issued covering the training of glider pilots stipulated that an applicant must have put in at least a hundred and fifty hours on Glider construction before he could be admitted to training. Girls were required to do half that number of hours on construction work, but the same total had to be made up in communal domestic duties.

We could feel satisfied with the results of our efforts in Finland. They were not sensational, but they formed bonds of real friendship, thanks to a common enthusiasm for gliding, our own genuine love for our task and, not least, to the fact that all our undertakings were successful and not a single mishap occurred during the whole of our stay. That fact alone earned us some admiration.

We arranged, for example, a Flying Day at a place about ninety miles from Helsinki, where, at that time, there was no smooth and level airfield we could use for a towed take-off, but only a clearing on the wooded slope of a hill and a stretch of heathland at its foot. Nevertheless, we succeeded in launching our gliders from the clearing and landing them again on the rough ground below.

For our next Flying Day, we chose a different site, the people flocking, as always, to watch the display. This time, we had an airfield. The day before, however, there had been torrential rain, turning the runway to a sea of mud and when we came to inspect it, our long boots simply sank in and stuck there. Any plane that had tried to take off or land in that morass would have finished up on its nose. It seemed a hopeless situation, till we thought of the paling fence that surrounded the airfield. We tore it up and laid the sections side by side along the ground, so making an airstrip firm enough for us to use.

Otherwise, our programme of demonstration flights and gliding instruction ran smoothly enough, each day finding us busy from early morning to late at night.

Our pupils comprised both civilians and soldiers and we assigned them to beginners' classes or advanced classes, the teaching of the beginners being infinitely the more exacting task. For our training, we had no towing planes and had to rely on winches.

In the winch take-off, the launching rope is attached to the drum of the winch at one side of the airfield and to the glider, at the other. The winch starts to rotate, drawing the glider towards it. Meanwhile, the pilot must keep the nose of the plane right up in an attitude of complete stall, like a kite, until the winch driver signals him to cast off the tow. But before he does so, the pilot must remember to put down the nose of the plane by pressing the stick forward—and that, for a beginner, requires some concentration.

In teaching this to my pupils, I learnt again how useful was the mental training in concentration which I had carried out when I was myself a beginner. The object was to learn, by repeatedly carrying them out in imagination, how to make the correct movements to control the plane absolutely automatically and without thinking, like a form of reflex action, in order to tide over the dangerous moment when the pilot is uncertain or afraid or for any other reason incapable of swift and lucid thought.

I left nothing undone to convince my pupils of the value of this training, or of the desirability of the object for which it was designed, and I went over with them again and again in our spare time the correct actions to be taken in various situations until, whatever the state of their emotions, they

could produce them with the certainty and regularity of
clockwork. Before each of my pupils took off during training
I would again go through these control movements with him
intensively.

By good luck—and by this means—there was not a crash
or an accident of any kind throughout the training courses
which we held in Finland.


## 12.  Pupil at a Civil Airways Training School

AT THE successful conclusion of the Finland expedition,
the Reich Air Ministry proposed to confer on us a
decoration, but as I laid no value on decorations, I asked,
instead, to be sent to the Civil Airways Training School in
Stettin. My flying permit had hitherto been restricted to
small, sports planes and here I should be able to satisfy my
wish to fly the larger types of aircraft.

My request was an unusual one, as at that time the Civil
Airways School took only male trainees and was run on
strict, semi-military lines. For a girl to go there would cause
a sensation, and, no doubt, a most unpleasant one. Nevertheless, my request was granted.

So I arrived in Stettin, little suspecting that the School
was staffed by officers to whom a woman on an airfield was
like a red rag to a bull. However, the Commandant, Colonel
Pasewald, determined to make the best of it, putting me
through the mill as decorously and as rapidly as possible.

On arrival I had to report to Colonel Pasewald. The interview was brief, on his side, a mixture of private advice and
soldierly instruction.

"So you have come here to join us?"

I nodded.

"You understand, I hope, what that means?"

I was silent.

"It means that you obey your duty orders. The course commences tomorrow, at 0600 hours . . ." etc., etc.

I was now caught up in a military mechanism that worked with alarming precision. Every time I took a step, I had the uneasy feeling that I was putting a foot wrong—as, indeed, I was!

On the morning of the first day of the course, we fell in to be mustered, according to height. With my five-feet-one I could hardly have claimed a preferential position in the line, but fortunately for me, we were first split into groups according to flying experience and, as I had already passed the course in Staaken, I was not forced to join the beginners' group at the end—a fact which caused me some secret satisfaction. But that could not prevent me from being the centre of interest and wherever I looked, I seemed to meet a grinning face. Everyone seemed to be expecting a highly entertaining time at my expense.

The Colonel appeared and with him the Major in charge of the course and a whole swarm of other people. The Commandant stationed himself in front of us and then proceeded to drill us.

I have forgotten most of the words of command, but I know that each one ran through me like an electric shock. As I looked round quickly and, as I thought, unobserved, to see what the others were doing, there came a roar from the front:
"Chest in!"

I was spoiling the dressing of the line. Naturally, there was a burst of laughter from the recruits and I took good care, from then on, to hold myself as stiff as a board so as to hear no more "Chest outs" or "Stomach ins," or whatever it was that was disturbing the splendours of the masculine silhouette.

Nevertheless, I continued to be singled out as an offender, for it naturally took some time for me to discover what I was supposed to do, to distinguish, for example, between "Eyes right" and "Right dress." Here again, I tried to copy the others, but it seemed impossible to conceal anything, even one's thoughts. I had to do extra drills—and it can be imagined what that meant before this forum. But I pulled myself together, determined not to be intimidated, for I felt, more than I knew, that they were only seeking an excuse to send me home.

But in course of time, my trials grew less, though I was never quite certain that some plot was not being hatched to trip me up, not out of malice but as part of a standing joke which kept officers as well as men continuously entertained. I took it all in good part, so that we all got on well together.

I was helped in the task of establishing myself by my flying experience, where I had an advantage over many of the other trainees. That I proved my capabilities in this sphere was, perhaps, the deciding factor in my finally being accepted without reserve on an equal footing with the men.

Looking back, I even believe that the presence of a girl who was as sincerely devoted to flying as any of them, far from having a disturbing influence in this life of Spartan discipline, acted as a kind of leaven, particularly as the discipline remained unimpaired. The proof was to be seen, not only in the attitude of the other trainees, but in that of the instructors, the officers and, above all, of the Commandant himself, with whose family I was soon on terms of friendship.

So, as the weeks flew past in Stettin, all thought of dropping me from the course was abandoned.

Then came the day when I was to pilot a twin-engined machine in a cross-country training flight. Colonel Pasewald gave me Cottbus as my goal. Cottbus had a Commandant who was liable to become violent at the mere thought of a "flying Fräulein." He and I were now to be involved in a little comedy for the amusement of Colonel Pasewald and his staff and before my departure, the Colonel therefore called me to his office.

"You are flying to Cottbus. Do you know the procedure for a cross-country flight?"

"Normally, yes—in this case, no."

It was true; our grim-faced Colonel actually laughed! Then he gave me "the drill":

On arrival at Cottbus I was to report to the station commander. I had to stand stiffly to attention and say:

"Flying pupil Hanna Reitsch of the German Civil Airways Training School Stettin reporting from the cross-country flight Stettin-Cottbus and return . . ."

Finding I was unable, at first, to recite this rigmarole, as required, right through without pause or mistake, I rehearsed my little speech during the flight to Cottbus until I found I could reel it off like a piece of tape. Naturally, I planned to make my entry—and my exit—a model of military correctitude, thereby attracting as little attention as possible.

As regards my outward appearance, I was completely confident. I was enveloped in a fur-lined flying-suit and it would be impossible to detect whether I was a boy or a girl. But it was too large for me in every dimension. The fur cap came so far down over my eyes that they were hardly visible. The boots were so large that, to keep them on my feet at all, I had had to stuff them with newspapers and other odds and ends. With my modest height, I looked in this get-up almost as broad as I was tall and the effect must have been grotesque in the extreme. There was one further point, my voice,—and I practiced speaking in a husky bass.

It was my sincere desire not to bring shame on my Training School and to that end I was determined to leave nothing undone. The crux of the matter, in my opinion, was to achieve the correct staccato effect of the genuine soldier. This, too, I hoped to perform with success.

On arrival at Cottbus, I went straight to the Commandant's office and, little suspecting his misogynist reputation, flicked and clicked my heels with truly warrior-like abandon before reciting my well rehearsed speech.

That over, there was a pause in which I indulged feelings of self-satisfaction. Then, with surprise, I noticed the adjutant staring at me, as though suddenly deprived of the vital principle of life. I had a strong feeling that it would be prudent to withdraw, and without delay, completely forgetting that I could not do so until the Commandant had dismissed me and knowing only that I felt an increasing urge to about-turn and "push off," as they say in soldiers' language.

So I turned on my heel, failing to notice that there was a strip of carpet on the floor, which now wound itself round my feet, bringing me full-length to the ground. Naturally, with all proper and soldierly speed, I attempted to get up again—to find my feet becoming ever more involved in the carpet and myself, still prostrate on the ground. As a roar of masculine laughter rang out above my head, I began to feel extremely foolish. Thank God, none of the Stettin boys had seen me in that situation, I would never have had a moment's peace!

When I landed again at Stettin, the story was already known to everyone, from the Colonel down to the youngest trainee on the course. I, on the other hand, believed that no one had heard about it and was determined to keep it a secret.

On landing, I was ordered to report to Colonel Pasewald. He received me in his room, surrounded by the officers of his staff, correct, as always, but in unaccountably jovial mood.

"Well, how was it?"

"Thank you, very nice."

Then I gave my report, advisedly skipping the story of my shame.

"No other incidents occurred? Well, out with it! Was that all? Nothing else to report?"

"What do you mean, what other incidents?"

"During the flight, for example?"

"No."

I was not sure what he was driving at. Did he know something, after all? Cautiously, I evaded his questions, so as not to lead him on to the track. It was like a gentle see-saw, a harmless game of cat and mouse, till, suddenly, they all burst out in a roar of laughter. Then I knew the game was up.

That incident made me doubly careful to avoid making further exhibitions of myself.

One day, I was allowed to fly my first aerobatics. Everyone

rejoiced with me at the prospect. The flying instructor took off with me in the double-decker "Stieglitz" and taught me to fly loops, turns and rolls. Then we landed and I took off again to try them alone. Blissfully, I flew a short distance from the airport and went into my first loop. Then I flew a second and a third and a whole series, one after another, in unbroken succession. After the loops, came the turns, after the turns, the rolls. I was glowing with enthusiasm, for here there was no one to say me nay, I could fly to my heart's content. But I was not performing the rolls correctly, I was somersaulting out of them. With a deafening roar, I went down and up, down again—and up, and this game I continued for a good half-hour without pause. Then I suddenly began to feel sick, so sick that at any moment——. In such situations, the only help is fresh air, so, sitting in an open machine, I hung my head out in the hope that I would feel better. But I could see that it was going to happen, whatever I did, though I just had time to realize that at all costs I must not be sick over the side, or when I landed they would be able to see the tell-tale marks on the fuselage. In a flash, I ripped off one glove, then the other: they were the only containers I could find . . .

When I landed, my comrades came hastening, friendly and solicitous, to congratulate me, casting, as they did so, a side-long glance at the fuselage,—spotless! They scrutinised my face—I did look a little off-colour, was I sure I felt all right? Yes, thank you, quite all right, it was not too bad at all. They winked at each other: "Don't worry, we'll catch her!"

Then they invited me to the canteen. This called for a celebration! Mountains of pastries were quickly piled on to my plate. The mere sight of them would have been enough to start my head swimming, had the disaster not already lain behind me. As it was, clear-eyed and ravenously hungry, I devoured every delicacy that was put before me. And my hosts had had to wait so long fo this moment—*quel dommage!*

## 13. Flying at Night

THE GERMAN Institute for Glider Research in Darmstadt had meanwhile acquired a Heinkel 46, a powered aircraft to be used for meteorological flights. After I had returned from Stettin, I was given the task of carrying out night flights in this machine, climbing every two hours to heights between six thousand and ten thousand feet, taking with me a "quintuplicator," an instrument that registers simultaneously wind strength, atmospheric pressure, humidity and temperature, together with the time at which they are recorded.

Every flight has its own unique beauty, but for me these first night-flights that I had ever made were especially wonderful.

I would take off at dusk, just as the red lights were switched on at the airfield to guide incoming planes. Then, in a glittering diadem, the lights of Darmstadt would drop into place below. Climbing higher, I would see Frankfurt twinkling in a double circlet against a velvet ground, then, farther away, more clusters of lights, seeming like mirrored reflections from the great and silent concourse of the stars.

When, after two hours, I took off again, climbing this time to nine thousand feet, the stillness was even more profound, while below the darkness had crept on, extinguishing all but, here and there, a solitary beacon at some station or public square. Two hours later, they, too, had gone.

At 4 a.m. I took off for the third time and now, the whole earth lay shrouded in soft night, while far above I soared alone, to the engine's rhythmic sound, through the limitless regions of the sky, my wings seeming like outstretched pinions guarding the slumbers of the world.

## 14. Across Europe to Lisbon

IN MAY, 1935, a popular festival took place in Lisbon, called the "Festivas Lisboa." Lasting for several days, the festival included a variety of exhibitions, entertainments and amusements and also, on this occasion, an International Air Display, during the course of which a demonstration was to be given of soaring flight.

Together with other glider pilots, I was asked to represent Germany in this event, and as a towing-plane would be required for our demonstrations, it fell to me to fly to Lisbon the small "Sport-Klemm" which had been chosen for the task. One of the glider pilots accompanied me as passenger while the remainder travelled by sea. Our route lay via Geneva, Lyons, Avignon, Perpignan, Barcelona and Madrid. In order to be able to see something of the country over which we passed, I planned to spread the flight over four days.

General peace-time conscription had recently been reintroduced in Germany and the international atmosphere was at that time extremely tense. I realised from the start, therefore, that considerable importance would attach, not only to our success in the air events in Lisbon and to our making an effective, though small contribution towards assuaging the general alarm, but also to the completion without incident of my flight across three international frontiers.

Before we started, I impressed on my companion the necessity of strict adherence to the instructions we had received, amongst others, that we were not to take any contraband articles with us, and he gave me his solemn and sacred promise not to do so.

When we reached Geneva, weather conditions were so bad that it seemed inadvisable to continue the flight. But I had no choice. I had to be in Barcelona by a definite date

89

and I had been told that at all costs I was to reach Lisbon in time for the Air Display. I left it to my companion, however, to choose whether he wished to come with me and he had no hesitation in deciding to do so.

We took off from Geneva amid torrential rain in a world that was grey upon grey. Beneath us, the Alps and the Jura lay blanketed in mist. Very cautiously, I "crept" through the mountain valleys until we descended into the plain on the outskirts of Lyons. Here visibility reduced to zero and the weather became so bad that any attempt to land in Lyons was out of the question. So, literally hopping over roofs and hedges, I decided to make for the nearest airfield.

On reaching one at last, I saw that it was a military airfield. Though, normally, I would not have been permitted to land there, I felt that in the circumstances I had no other choice. As soon as we had touched down and come to a stop, I asked my companion to allow me to do the talking, as with my better knowledge of French I would be less likely to create some unfortunate misunderstanding.

Having recognised the swastika on the plane, a number of French officers came running up in a state of considerable agitation. I asked to be taken to the Commandant and we were duly conducted to his office.

The Commandant greeted us with extreme reserve. I apologised for having landed without permission and attempted to explain the situation. When I had finished, he was a changed man. With the utmost charm and courtesy, he expressed, after the chivalrous manner of his race, the most lively sympathy for us in our predicament and assured us that he regretted having to do so, but unfortunately duty left him no choice—it would be necessary to have our baggage examined to confirm that were were not carrying any prohibited articles.

What articles were prohibited?

"Well, for example, photographic equipment."

"No," I said emphatically, "I can give you my word that we have nothing like that with us."

Escorted by some soldiers, we were then sent to the airfield to collect our luggage. On the way back I remembered that I had forgotten something and returned to the plane to fetch it. When, later than the others, I entered the barrack, I was confronted with an icy silence: with quick, angry little steps, the Commandant marched up and stationed himself before me:

"You say you are not carrying photographic apparatuses?"

"No."

Immediately, as though the word had touched some hidden reflex, the Commandant produced and held before my eyes—a Leica camera!

My companion was an excellent glider pilot and had, I knew, been given the Leica as a prize in one of the Rhön Soaring Contests. But, angered by his action which had already shown me to be an obvious liar and a probable spy and might have further, even more serious repercussions, I felt that a demonstration of sentimental comradeship would be both unwise and out of place and determined to plant the guilt fairly and squarely on the shoulders to which it belonged.

I therefore assured the Commandant that I had known nothing about the camera and that we had, in fact, been given strict instructions not to take any photographic equipment with us, but that my colleague had never been abroad before and for that reason, presumably, had failed to appreciate the gravity of his action.

Listening without comment, the Commandant now proceeded to examine our hand luggage, finding in my companion's brief-case—blue-prints and specifications of aircraft . . .

At this, I thought for a moment that I was going to faint. Though I knew that my passenger was a student at the Technische Hochschule and was about to sit for his Diploma, I was also well aware that in the present circumstances the explanation would sound neither credible nor adequate.

The Commandant, indeed, would listen to no further explanations from me of any kind and it was obvious whom he considered to be the real culprit. Meanwhile overwhelmed and prostrated with shame, my colleague was

sitting, speechless, in a corner of the room and his state of
moral collapse seemed to make, if anything, a favourable
impression,—if such a possibility could still be said to exist.
As for me, it was clear that my attempts at explanation were
interpreted as no more than a spirited piece of play-acting
and that I was looked on as a peculiarly resourceful and
dangerous customer.

The Commandant's worst suspicions seemed to be confirmed when he examined our papers and discovered that
my companion was also a pilot—conclusive evidence that I,
in fact, was no pilot at all but a spy.

Though I tried not to show it, I was now in despair, unable
to see how we could ever manage to extricate ourselves. At
the same time, I was determined, come what might, not to
abandon my appointed flight-schedule.

Our situation now deteriorated still further when, on the
Commandant's orders, the doors were locked and we were
placed under armed guard. Some officers took it in turns to
interrogate us. This was the first military cross-examination
which I had been called upon to withstand and it seemed a
terrible ordeal. Not until 1945 did I realise that interrogation
could assume far more subtle and unpleasant forms.

At first I failed to notice the skill and care with which the
questions had been prepared. I even imagined that I would
be able to direct the conversation, until the ambiguity of
each question made me realise that I was not the leader but
the led. As, however, I stood before my judges with a completely clear conscience, no manoeuvre, however skilfully
contrived, could succeed in cornering me.

But they could and would prevent me and my companion
from continuing our flight. In course of conversation, I learnt
that our plane was to be dismantled and searched. That
would mean days or even weeks of delay before it was
restored to us. Meanwhile, the festivities in Lisbon would
have taken place without the participation of Germany, for,
apart from the absence of my companion and myself, without
the towing plane, the whole gliding programme would have
to be cancelled.

I was asked whether any of our possessions were still in the plane and I remembered some air maps. The interrogating officer instructed me to fetch them and detailed a soldier to escort me to the plane.

Meanwhile, the rumour had got about that two German spies had landed and were under arrest and when we came on to the airfield, we found a large and sensation-hungry assortment of troops and civilians: Moroccans, blacks, half-whites and whites. I had never seen so colourful a collection but was left no time to gaze at them for, as my guard and I approached, they began to spit at me as a spy and use foul epithets, not confining themselves to my person but attacking as well the German Government with harsh and provocative abuse.

I could only continue towards the plane, making a passage for myself quietly but firmly through the throng. As I climbed in to fetch the maps, the abuse was sustained without pause, even following us on our return journey across the airfield. I was white with rage but refrained from speaking so as not to make matters worse. In every nerve I felt the humiliation of my predicament, though I was spared all reason for shame.

But the little French soldier who accompanied me felt shamed and embarrassed by his compatriots' behaviour.

"We young fellows can understand you," he said, "because you are young in Germany. These people are old and blind."

I felt better for these words of human feeling and felt, also, a ray of hope.

"You must help me," I said. "You must arrange for me to telephone."

I said no more and he made no reply.

After I had returned to the barrack, my colleague and I were asked after a while if we would like something to eat. He said he was not hungry but as it was now afternoon and I had eaten nothing all day, I gladly accepted, particularly as I suspected that my small friend had something to do with it. Under his escort, I was now sent to the canteen, which was empty at this time of day. I took the opportunity to ask him

if he would try and get the German Consul in Lyons for me
on the telephone. Surprisingly enough, he agreed to try and
succeeded in getting through.

The Consul had just returned to his office, having spent
some hours waiting for us at the airport. He had learnt that
we had taken off from Geneva in spite of the weather and,
after a time, there still being no further news of us, had
informed the rescue service so that a search could be made.
He was therefore greatly relieved to hear that we were safe
and had actually landed in the neighbourhood of Lyons.

His good humour rapidly evaporated, however, as I told
him the remainder of our story and he began to discharge a
series of loud and incomprehensible sounds into the telephone from which I gathered that he was beside himself with
fury and fright. That, however was his own affair and I contented myself with asking him to come out to us at once, as a
matter of urgency, and then hung up.

After the meal, the interrogation was continued. They
were taking a lot of trouble with me, I thought with some
embitterment, although in fairness I had to admit that, from
their point of view, they had every reason to do so. In the
knowledge that something was at last going to happen, I at
any rate now felt considerably more at ease.

In half an hour, the Commandant was called to the telephone.

When, after some considerable time, he returned, there,
standing before us, was once more the charming and con-
siderate officer we had originally known: and this time,
moreover, he apologised. He told us that the French Ministry
of Aviation itself had intervened with an order for our
immediate release.

Now it was his turn to be concerned lest the incident
should have political repercussions and he made strenuous
efforts to erase the unfavourable impressions of the last few
hours. But I had only one wish—to see the last of the place.

The machine was cleared to take off. Naturally, the Commandant and his entourage accompanied us to the airfield.
Somewhere, I happened to catch sight of my little French

soldier; he, I felt, deserved to be given a treat, so I asked the Commandant if, before we left, I might give him a joy-ride as a token of gratitude for his timely act of assistance.

The delight of the little fellow was great. As I strapped him in, I told him that I proposed to fly the machine to the limit of her performance and asked for his agreement. Then we took off and the machine showed what she could do: down in a dive, so close to the ground that the wheels almost brushed the grass, then straight as an arrow at the group of bystanders, who threw themselves to the ground before, at the last second, I pulled up the nose and, to finish off with, a nicely executed turn!

My passenger seemed to have suffered no ill effects and stepped out of the plane beaming with joy. We then took our leave of the officers who seemed as pleased as we were at this friendly conclusion to the whole unhappy affair and, my German colleague having taken his place in the plane, we then continued our journey.

We reached the civil airport at Lyons before dark and I went to see the German Consul. It was not easy to pacify him and I had to spend most of the night in discussion, explanation and argument.

We took off again from Lyons in the early hours and continued as far as Avignon, where I had to land for petrol. Having filled up, I asked my colleague to pay, as he was responsible for the financial side of our journey and had all our money. Our trip to Lisbon had been arranged at the last moment and there had been no time for more than the bare minimum of foreign currency to be obtained to cover our petrol requirements and it was therefore better that one of us should keep the money and control expenditure than that we should share it between us. I handed over this responsibility to my colleague all the more willingly, in that I was inexperienced in such matters.

He, therefore, had now to pay for the petrol. He put his hand in his pocket,—no purse. He searched his other pockets,—still no purse! He went over them all again, then, nervously, all over again, but, however often he plunged his hand in, still, obstinately, the purse declined to come to light—till at last he had to admit that he had lost it.

So now, as well as a spy, I was a cheat.

But the pump attendant proved neither obstinate nor truculent and allowed us credit until, in a fortnight's time, we could pay the account on our return journey. Meanwhile, I gave him an I.O.U. which, if need be, he could redeem at the German Consulate in Lyons.

That obstacle we had surmounted, but there was another to come. Before reaching Barcelona, we would have to land again for petrol in Perpignan. Being off the main air routes, the airfield there was very little used and our arrival proved quite an event. This lightened my unpleasant task of having to refuel without money. The pump attendant turned out to be the local shepherd and he accepted the situation with philosophical calm, never doubting that in God's good time, the money would be paid. Thanks to him, we arrived in Barcelona according to schedule.

The air displays in Lisbon were for organisers and participants a complete success. Some magnificent performances were given, while the company of the great fliers of other nations heightened the pleasure of the whole event and added to the zest of one's share in it. Our minds were in harmony, untouched by the tensions of the outside world, for common to us all was the one overmastering desire—to soar in the beauty of flight.

But beside these, Lisbon was to provide other happy experiences. I have already mentioned that the "Festivas Lisboa" represented a kind of popular Portuguese festival. An exhibition town, "Old Lisbon," had been specially built for the occasion, in which the houses were built in old Portuguese style and the inhabitants dressed in costumes of the period. There was a mediaeval prison and mediaeval justice was supposed to prevail in the town.

I wanted to see this town and asked a Portuguese couple who were friends of mine to accompany me. As I had come straight from the plane, I was still in my flying clothes, consisting of slacks and short red jacket. In Germany they would have passed unnoticed but I had forgotten that Portuguese custom requires women to be dressed in public with the utmost reticence. In 1935, for a woman to be seen wearing trousers in the streets was unheard-of.

As we entered the exhibition area, therefore, I was quickly spotted and before long we were being followed by a swarm of vociferous and applauding flying enthusiasts. Among them were two soldiers, mercenaries in mediaeval costume. Pushing their way through the throng, they descended on me with the curt announcement that, having appeared in the public streets in pyjamas, thereby challenging the customary standards of decorum and seemly deportment, I had rendered myself liable to suffer the utmost rigours of the law —and was now under arrest.

I felt uncomfortable and confused. Was it a joke or were they in earnest? I was not sure and appealed for help to my Portuguese friends. Their only counsel was not to be a spoilsport.

I was now led to a tiny, narrow cell, completely bare except for a wooden bench and a pitcher of water. The door swung to behind me. The crowd that had followed us now gradually dispersed and I was left alone with my thoughts. Doubts and conjectures began to chase through my mind: after all, as a member of the German delegation, had I not been told to avoid provoking unpleasant incidents?

After a while, I again heard footsteps approaching. Again, a stream of people filed past, peering curiously through the grille at the foreign prisoner. I now bitterly regretted having entered the jest.

Shortly after, the two soldiers returned to lead me before the tribunal. I was taken to a marquee crammed with people. At the far end, sat a white-bearded judge in a long, black gown, before him was a bench for the prisoner and on either side a row of benches for the witnesses.

I was led to the prisoner's bench, where my defending counsel already awaited me. A bell was rung and immediately a deathly hush fell on the assembly.

My counsel opened the proceedings. In a long and
elegant discourse, he professed himself honoured at being
entrusted with the defence of an aviator whose name would
already be well known to his hearers. He said a great deal
more, to conclude, finally, by laying down his mandate on
the grounds that the offence which I had committed was too
serious to allow of any atonement. He then abandoned me
to the mercy of the Court. The audience signified their
approval with thunderous applause.

With due solemnity the judge now rose and proceeded to
address the Court. First, he outlined the facts of the case and
drew attention to the severity of the offence. Then, turning to
me, he dealt with the prisoner's record, speaking with such a
skilful mixture of fantasy and truth that I began to think he
knew more about me than I did myself. At any rate, it was
now clear that I was taking part in a brilliant and charming
comedy and I felt greatly relieved, as well as pleased to think
that I had not spoilt the amusement.

The judge spoke not only of me but of Germany and the
German people, whom he praised for their courage and
energy in rising again after their defeat in war. Can it be
wondered that I felt happy and proud?

From earnest, he now turned to jest again, asserting that
the virtues which he had just singled for praise made it
impossible for him to sentence me. Finally, he called upon
the public to rise in salutation to myself and to the German
people.

As I left the tent, my hand was almost numbed with the
congratulations that were pressed upon me, but I hardly felt
it in my gratitude to this charming and friendly people.

For my return to Germany, I took the same route that my
companion and I had followed on the way out. But this time,
he travelled by sea.

In Barcelona, I was accorded a particularly hearty welcome and, breaking my journey, spent a few pleasant days
there. As everywhere on my return flight, I found a large
number of people assembled to see me off, not only personal

1.  Hanna Reitsch at the Wasserkuppe gliding competition, in the 1930s.

2. Hanna Reitsch's glider, *Reiher (Heron)*, in the Wasserkuppe gliding competition.

3. Hanna Reitsch's Training Glider: a photograph taken before the war.

4. Being helped into the cockpit by Wolf Hirth, who taught her gliding.

5. With her parents in front of the Town Hall at Hirschberg, following the presentation of a Scroll of Honorary Citizenship, April 1941.

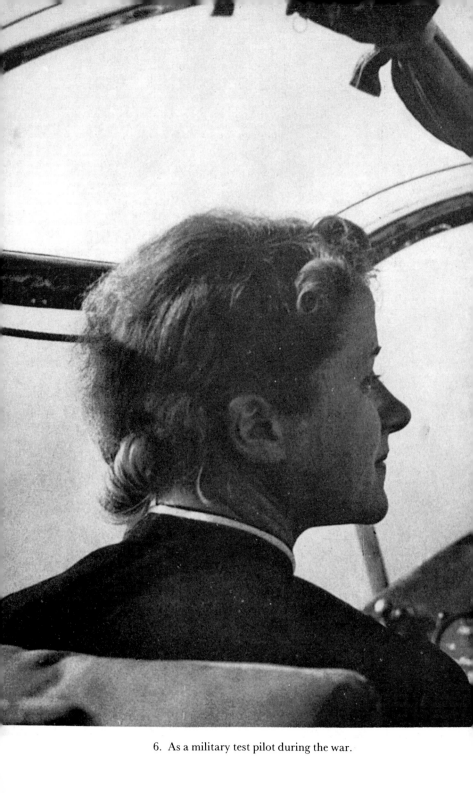

6. As a military test pilot during the war.

7. In 1944, with war decorations.

8. With Ernst Udet.

9. *(left)* Hanna Reitsch
with her mother.

10. *(below)* Her father.

11. With Professor Willy Messerschmitt (left) and Professor Alexander Lippisch during the test flights for Me 163b, October 1942.

12. Returning from the front in a He 111.

13. *(above)* Before the V1 was adapted as a human glider-bomb, Hanna Reitsch experimented with an engineless Me 328, launched in mid-air from a mother-plane.

14. *(below)* A Dornier 17, equipped for cutting barrage balloon cables.

15. *(above)* The *Sea Eagle*, the first flying boat glider. Hanna Reitsch directs the crane as she is lifted out after the first experimental trials.

16. *(below)* One of the most hazardous testing operations carried out by Hanna Reitsch, was to land on a "bed of ropes" in a glider. It was intended to develop this method of landing for use by small observation planes on board ship.

17. *(above)* The rocket-propelled Messerschmitt Me 163b which shot up to 30,000 feet in 90 seconds. Hanna Reitsch was seriously injured during experimental work in this aircraft.

18. *(below)* The V1 flying bomb, as launched against London, etc., from sites in France and elsewhere.

19. *(above)* The piloted "suicide" version of the V1.

20. *(below)* The two-seat version of the V1 flying bomb, without power unit, in which prospective suicide pilots were trained.

21. Hanna Reitsch.

friends, but gliding enthusiasts, representatives of public offices and official organisations.

At Barcelona, I was so engrossed in conversation with these well-wishers, that I paid little attention when I was asked for my "Carnet de Passage," or log-book, so that it could be stamped with my exit from Spanish territory, but merely handed it over, putting it straight back into my pocket when it was returned to me. Then I took off on a wonderful flight over the Pyrenees.

In France, I had to land again at Perpignan to refuel and also to repay my debts. The pump attendant was overjoyed to see me, especially as he had read meanwhile in the French newspapers about our activities in Lisbon. As this was the first point which I touched on French soil during my return flight, it fell to him to make the necessary entry in my log-book, a task which he performed with the utmost solemnity and zeal. While he was so engaged, I happened to glance over his shoulder—to receive a terrible shock. The identifying letters of my plane were "D-EJEN," but there, on the page before him, in clear, bold letters, stood: "D-AJEX," and then: "Pilot and owner of aircraft: Dr. W——, Stuttgart." The official in Barcelona had given me the wrong log-book . . .

My first thought was that, at all costs, I must conceal the mistake from the friendly shepherd and pump attendant, for once he had spotted it, he would be sure to become the full-blown customs official and would hold me here indefinitely until the whole matter had been carefully regularised.

So, on the pretext that my next landing would be in Switzerland, I asked him if he would stamp not only my entry into France but also my exit. I knew that the latter conferred on him the right to examine my luggage and I guessed—as it proved, correctly—that he would find that opportunity too good to be missed. In this way, I managed to divert his attention from the fatal "Carnet de Passage."

My next landing was in Avignon. Here the photos of the gliding events in Lisbon could play their part. While still in flight, I slipped them between the pages of the log-book, to

present the whole lot, on arrival at Avignon, to the official
who asked for my papers. As I had expected, he first examined the photos and I had to give him a detailed account of
everything that had transpired in Lisbon. But the critical
moment arrived at last and he began to examine the log-
book. Here again, luck came to my aid and he looked no
further than the entries which had already been made in
Perpignan. I was free to continue my flight.

In Lyons, I had again to land and refuel. This time, so as
to be certain of being able to leave next morning without
difficulty, I spent the night in the customs compound.

But there was one more hurdle—Geneva. There my luck
deserted me. The official who dealt with me scrupulously
avoided speaking one word of German and conscientiously
examined every single entry in the log-book.

"So you decided to change planes en route?"

"No."

"Your machine over there is "D-EJEN." In the book here
it says "D-AJEX.""

"Let me see."

He showed me the entry.

"That isn't my book!"

"Oh, so it isn't your book?"

"No, it isn't," I said. "Look here: 'D-AJEX,' instead of
'D-EJEN.' 'Type: Siemens-Motor,' mine is a Hirth-
Klemm . . .""

So I went on, point by point: I thought I was never going
to convince him. But at last he had to admit, the plane was
mine, but the famous "Carnet de Passage" was not.

Once this was established, his whole manner altered.
Intent now on the amazing fact that his French colleagues in
Perpignan, Avignon and Lyons had failed to detect the
mistake, he was too pleased to worry about how it had
arisen. To me, he was generous in the extreme and after
confirming my particulars by radio with Barcelona, he
cleared me to take off.

My next touch-down was in Germany, at Freiburg. Home
at last! Yes,—but with the wrong log-book . . . And now,

once again in dear, old Germany, no explanations of mine
were of the slightest avail. Regulations were regulations and
the matter would have to take its course. So in Freiburg I
stayed, until the last, mountainous obstacle had been
officially removed and I was free to return to Darmstadt.

## 15.  Test-Gliding

WHEN I first joined the Institute for Glider Research,
my duties were of a general kind, but in 1935 I became
a member of the Department, under the direction of Hans
Jacobs, that specialised in gliding and soaring.

My appointment was due to a stroke of good fortune. The
well-known airman, Ludwig Hoffmann, had originally been
chosen as test-pilot for the Institute but as a serious illness
prevented him from taking up the appointment, I was asked
to take his place.

Though I brought to my new task plenty of resolve and
enthusiasm, my technical knowledge, including that of aircraft construction, was non-existent and I had, at first, to
rely on my flying instinct and my capacity for observation.

In what, then, in simple terms, does the task of the test-
pilot consist?

The testing of new types of planes, both powered aircraft
and gliders, or of some modification to an existing design,
naturally involves an increased element of risk, for the pilot
is introducing the aircraft for the first time into its element
and in spite of every care taken in design and construction,
the possibility of defects leading to failure of the aircraft can
not be excluded. Longitudinal stability, for example, may be
inadequate, so that the plane can not be maintained on a
level course, or some part of the superstructure may cause
the air-stream to be deflected, resulting in vibration or in

rocking movements, so that the pilot is powerless to prevent the eventual failure of some vital component. Naturally, he will attempt to reduce the air-speed, but these phenomena tend to occur with such suddenness that his efforts are often too late to save the plane. In that event, his only recourse is to bale out, but that is not always an easy matter when the plane is falling at an increasing speed.

But the conscientious test-pilot will test his plane step by step, so that he only gradually approaches the danger zone and he will not, for example, attempt to reach maximum speed on his first flight. Eddies in the air-stream can usually be detected by a slight quivering in the stick and control surfaces, but the test-pilot is required, not only to notice that such phenomena are taking place, but also, if possible, to establish their source, and this calls for acute powers of observation.

In subsequent discussion with the aircraft constructor and the specialist in aerodynamics, the test-pilot will then attempt to find the cause of the defects so that the necessary modifications can be made, for example, improvement in the design of a fairing, a more effectively balanced rudder, the elimination of play in the controls or of excessive softness in the rudder.

Having satisfied himself that the plane performs faultlessly at the designed speeds in normal altitudes of flight, the test-pilot will then proceed to test it in all other attitudes, on its back, when rotating on its longitudinal axis, that is, in rolls, and when looping both forwards as well as backwards. Only when all these aspects of an aircraft's performance have been found satisfactory, can the more sensitive adjustments be undertaken, for example, the equation of control-load with control-efficiency, in which the reduction of friction in control wires play an important part.

It would take too long to list everything that a test-pilot has to check and, where necessary, to rectify during the trial of a single aircraft. The tests are seldom completed in a matter of days and may even last for several months, continuing sometimes after mass-production of the aircraft has already started, so that improvements can be introduced with the minimum of delay.

The test-pilot's work is not confined to new types only. In the case of a crash, for example, in which the pilot has lost his life through no apparent error on his part, the production of that particular type of plane may be suspended until the precise reason for the disaster is known. To discover this is the joint task of the designer and the test-pilot and a very laborious and dangerous process it can be. After scrutinising every available eye-witness account, the test-pilot will attempt to put an identical aircraft through the same series of manoeuvres that preceded the crash,—at a very high altitude, so that, if structural or mechanical failure occurs, he can make use of his parachute.

A further duty of a test-pilot may be to submit some accepted type of aircraft to special tests for research purposes. I will return to this subject later.

The first aircraft which I was called upon to test, at the Institute for Glider Research, was the new sailplane called the "Crane."

Every day, while the "Crane" had been under construction, I have been in the workshops, getting to know the controls, the field of vision, the amount of space which I shall have as pilot, until I can say that I am already part of the plane—when it is on the ground.

But so far, I have flown it in imagination only, have only been able to guess what effects the movements of the rudder will have, how the plane will behave in the air. So my first flight will be a cautious one.

Now, tense in every nerve, I am waiting on the airfield for the take-off. The workmen and technicians have come from the shops and are standing about, waiting, no less tensely, for the moment when their bird first leaves the ground.

The tug is in position, the towing-cable is made fast and a man stations himself at a wing-tip to keep my plane on a straight course.

Now the plane in front of me opens up, the rope starts to

heave and the "Crane" to roll faster and faster over the
ground. At first, the man runs with me, still holding the
wing-tip, but now he drops behind and, at the same
moment, I feel enough pressure on the stick to balance the
wings. So I am air-borne, a few feet only off the ground.

At no more than twenty feet, so that, if need be, I can drop
the tow and land immediately, I start to test the aircraft's
stability, round its lateral axis with the elevator, its longitudinal axis with the ailerons and its vertical axis with the
rudder.

As soon as I am satisfied that the aircraft is stable and can
be controlled without danger, I allow myself to be towed to
higher altitudes, climbing up gently until I reach a sufficient
height to be able to bale out in the event of unpleasant
surprises.

Casting off the tow at 6,500 feet, I first proceed to obtain
an overall impression of the plane. Is there an adequate field
of vision? Can the rudder be moved without undue effort?
Does the plane answer smartly to the rudder? Then I
experiment cautiously to discover the aircraft's stalling angle,
that is, at what angle of incidence of the wings and at what
part of their leading edge, the airflow first begins to break
away from their upper surface. If this phenomenon starts at
a wing-tip, the plane will tilt slightly to one side and go into a
spin. Does the wing drop suddenly or gradually? Can the
spin be easily corrected?

These questions can only be answered by cautious explora-
tion combined with the most intense and concentrated
attention to every sound and movement made by the plane
and, in so doing, I have steadily been losing height until now
I must come into land.

Below, the designer, the draughtsmen and the constructors
are anxiously waiting for my report, but at first there is
nothing but joy that this first flight has been successfully
concluded. Then, soberly, we set to work once more. My
observations are discussed, the necessary modifications
decided upon and the details passed to the workshops.

As soon as the modifications have been completed, I take

off again. And so it continues, flight after flight, each time reaching a higher speed, each higher speed bringing, possibly, some further defect or weakness to light until my duty is fulfilled to test the plane to its uttermost limits, in rough weather as well as smooth, so that when I finally hand it over, no further surprises can occur.

It would take too long to describe every test which I carried out for the Glider Research Institute and I will confine myself, therefore, to one or two further examples, illustrating both the variety and the intricate, responsible and exacting nature of a test-pilot's work.

After testing the "Crane," I was called upon, in the summer of 1935, to test the "Sea Eagle," the first glider-seaplane designed by Hans Jacobs.

Though the idea of an amphibian glider was not new, the "Sea Eagle" represented the first attempt to construct a high-performance plane of this type, for use, principally, in scientific research expeditions.

The first test, carried out on the Chiemsee, south-east of Munich, was abortive, the motor-boat which had been procured to act as tow being unable to reach the take-off speed. We then transferred to the Bodensee, where the Maybach speed-boat which Dornier placed at our disposal proved adequate to the task.

That may sound simple but in reality, the problem of the take-off proved both difficult and dangerous. We used, at first, a three hundred foot tow-rope, but its weight and resistance in the water were so great that, when I took off and rose to a height of about thirty feet, the rope dragged me down again sharply and I quickly cast off for fear I would strike the water and break up.

Watching from the boat, my friends, however, were of the opinion that I should have held on and so I tried a second time, doing as they suggested until there came a sudden jar, a sheet of water swept up over the plane and together we dived below like a submarine—to surface again, a few seconds later, completely unharmed.

Though this experience supplied conclusive evidence of the solidity of the machine's construction, my friends were unanimous in considering it unsatisfactory as a permanent method of taking off.

The tow-rope was now shortened to 230 feet and provided with small, stream-lined floats made of balsa wood. In this way, I could take off in the "Sea Eagle" without immediately being dragged down again. This device proved practicable, even to the limit of the weather conditions which the speed-boat could tolerate.

Thereafter, we continued the tests, using a Dornier amphibian flying-boat, the "Dragon-Fly" as tow. This was lent to us, together with a pilot, by a well-known aircraft manufacturing firm.

The pilot, Sepp Gertis, proved to be excellent at the task of towing, particularly when we were determining the worst weather conditions in which he could operate the "Dragon-Fly," an undertaking which he carried out with an admirable mixture of caution and cold-blooded daring.

As for me, I found it a great advantage that the slip-stream of the amphibian's airscrew left a comparatively calm strip of water in the wake of the plane on which I could hold the "Sea Eagle" with ease, even in wind conditions which forced the towing plane to battle against the waves. The take-off when on tow behind the Dornier amphibian proved equally straightforward.

I allowed myself to be towed to a considerable height before casting off.

The weather forecast predicted storm and the clouds were already gathering in the sky. But this was the very weather we had hoped for, so that we could test the behaviour of the "Sea Eagle" when landing on rough water. Every kind of lifesaving device stood ready for my use on shore, though my thoughts did not lie, at the moment, in that direction!

First, I searched round for a cloud which would ensure me an up-wind. I soared up, struggling continually against the approaching storm, so as not to be driven too far from my landing target.

Below me, the foam crests of the waves were steadily increasing and all boats had long ago returned for shelter to the shore.

I must have been soaring for a good hour before I came down to land. The "Sea Eagle" had a hull like a boat and, at a landing-speed of barely 35 m.p.h., I touched her gently down on the water. Immediately, the waves began to throw the plane about as they rolled up, peak upon trough, in an endless succession. But the plane rode them out, placid and unruffled by the fury of the elements.

No boats were able to put out to fetch us and for such occasions, the aircraft hangars which stood at the water's edge were fitted with cranes. I found that the only way to fasten the hook of the crane on to the aircraft was for me to stand on one of the wings in order to help keep her on an even keel. But all went well and the "Sea Eagle" was hoisted in without damage. The plane had certainly withstood its baptism and with that, our task was completed.

From the Bodensee, we then returned to the Chiemsee to test a new catapult launching device. This, the so-called Madelung catapult, was intended to enable heavily laden transport planes to take off in a small space instead of from the immensely long runway that was normally required. The catapult had already been tested on land and it was now a matter of establishing whether it would prove equally useful for a water take-off. For these tests, the "Sea-Eagle" was considered a suitable plane.

The catapult was set up on the shores of the lake. In essentials, it consisted of a device to transfer to the aircraft the energy of a rotating fly-wheel by means of a steel rope led over a cone-shaped drum.

As the rope was taken up by the drum at an increasing speed, it snatched me and my glider directly towards the scaffolding of the catapult erected on shore. The feeling was distinctly unpleasant. The crux of the matter was to wait for precisely the right moment at which to drop the tow, then to perform a neat and rapid turn and land again on the water. As in so many tests, this task called for the greatest care and concentration if disaster was to be avoided.

The trials were successfully concluded, so paving the way for further tests with powered aircraft.

Our work at the Institute consisted not only of testing new types of aircraft but also of improving existing types. If, for example, some particular design of glider had been involved in a succession of fatal accidents, its certificate of airworthiness would first be suspended by the Directorate of Air Safety and then a machine of that type sent to us at the Institute for examination.

During the year 1936, an increased number of fatal crashes occurred through glider pilots with inadequate experience of blind-flying attempting flights in cloud, with the result that they imposed too great a strain on their machines. The latter then broke up, often in circumstances which prevented their pilots from using their parachutes.

In due course, the German Experimental Station for Aeronautical Research in Berlin-Adlershof intervened with an order that new specifications for the structural stability of glider aircraft should be prepared.

But Hans Jacobs, the Chief Designer and Director of the Institute, taking the view that any aircraft, no matter how strong its construction, could be made to break up under sufficiently brutal and irresponsible treatment, decided against increasing the structural rigidity, which would be certain to entail a considerable reduction in performance, and chose, instead, to fit a braking device, with the double object of increasing the aircraft's stability and setting a definite limit to its maximum speed, even when put into a vertical dive. For this purpose, he fitted self-operating dive brakes on the upper and lower surface of each wing, one set opening with the wind and the other set, against it. For the tests, we selected the "Sperber" glider.

Imagine, then, I am taking off in clear weather and, at a height of 13,000 feet, cast off the tow and operate the brakes at moderate speed. Immediately, the glider begins to lose height and speed so that, almost without thinking, I move the elevator to counteract their effect. Then, with the brakes still open, I dive, slowly increasing speed,—5 m.p.h. faster—10 m.p.h., and now the strong turbulence set up by the brakes that are open into the wind starts to buffet the ailerons and the elevator so that the whole plane begins to shudder. I press myself against the side of the plane and listen, every sense alert to try and determine the source and cause of the vibration. Then I close the brakes for a moment while I note down briefly what I have heard, felt and seen. Then, increasing the speed, I open the brakes once more and, as expected, the vibration is now so strong that the control column is torn out of my hands. Clearly the dive brakes are unsatisfactory in their present form, so I land and discuss with Hans Jacobs what I have observed. To reduce the disturbance which they make in the slip-stream, we decide to dampen the brakes with a series of holes and slots.

So, day after day, week after week, the tests continue and each morning a letter from my mother accompanies me, giving me complete peace of mind. So deep is her conviction that I am in God's hand and that nothing can ever happen to me except by His Will, that her faith gradually becomes a part of myself. If my end is in His Will, then my end will overtake me, even in the safest corner of the globe. I can feel how, through her thoughts, I am positively compelled to an attitude of humble readiness.

She knows that I live to fly. She knows how much I love my life, my work, the tests on which I am engaged. But greater than the danger of flying is, to her, the danger that success can bring and she never tires of warning me against the blindness of vanity and overweening pride.

And there is something further that she expresses, in the letters that she writes to me at night, when the household have gone to bed: the happiness that she shares with me in knowing that every test we carry out is in the cause of Germany and the saving of human lives.

Meanwhile, gliding at heights between 14,000 and 19,000

feet, I continue to experiment with the new dive-brakes until, at last, the final phase arrives—to test them in a vertical dive.

I have learnt by experience that though the plane may remain steady at a high speed, only a minute increase in that speed may suddenly produce severe wing flutter. If that were to occur during a vertical dive, the machine might not withstand the strain. For a moment, I am tempted to land and postpone the last test until tomorrow. After all, I don't have to do it. And then, suddenly, while my attention is still concentrated on the plane, I see the picture of my mother before me. She feels, I know, more strongly than anything, that I must live the life that has been allotted to me, and so, tense in every nerve, I put the plane into a vertical dive and hold her there, through 7,000—8,000—9,000 feet, while the machine, all the while as steady as a board, never once exceeds the speed of 125 miles per-hour.

At about 600 feet I flatten out, close the dive brakes and land, and while the blood is still thumping in my temples, Hans Jacobs, Professor Georgii, my fellow pilots and the aircraft fitters come running up, overjoyed, to offer their congratulations. We have achieved our object.

Though, in the Twentieth Century, the flood of new inventions has been such, that today's wonder is tomorrow's platitude, nevertheless, the introduction of dive brakes as a result of our tests in 1936 proved to be an important milestone in the history of aeronautics—however difficult it may be to realise, for us who are accustomed to think in terms of rocket planes, jets and stratocruisers.

After the successful conclusion of the tests, a demonstration of the dive brakes took place, at the instigation of Professor Georgii, before Udet, General von Greim and other Luftwaffe generals at the airfield at Darmstadt-Griesheim.

Duly impressed by the effectiveness of the brakes as a safety device, Udet wished to see them fitted to certain military aircraft and at his request, therefore, I repeated my demonstration in the Spring of 1937 before the chief designers of the leading German aircraft manufacturers. Here, too, this first experience of seeing a glider go into a vertical dive left a deep impression on my audience and, as a consequence, the Institute for Glider Research acquired a new interest and importance in the eyes of those officially concerned in Germany with aeronautical development.

After my demonstration in Darmstadt-Griesheim, Udet conferred on me—the first woman ever to receive it—the honorary title of "Flugkapitän." The title had previously been bestowed, upon the completion of certain prescribed conditions, exclusively on pilots of the Lufthansa, the German Civil Airways, but my appointment now set the precedent for its extension to include pilots engaged in aeronautical research.

## 16.  A Bird Soars Over the Alps

IN MAY, 1937, there were newspaper headlines: "GERMAN PILOTS' TRIUMPHANT SUCCESS—5 GERMANS FIRST EVER TO CROSS ALPS BY SAILPLANE"; and I was one of them.

My plane was a Sperber Junior, constructed, or rather "tailored" by Hans Jacobs to fit me exactly, and so exactly, that once in the pilot's seat even I could hardly move, while only I could get into it at all. So much did I feel a part of the plane, that the wings seemed to grow out of my shoulders.

In Salzburg, that month, the International Study Commission for Motorless Flight was sitting under the chairmanship of Professor Georgii and, coinciding with it, a meeting of international glider pilots was to be held. For the latter, a series of competitions had been arranged, point-to-point flights, cross-country flights and altitude flights, during the course of which we were to penetrate as far as we could into the area of the High Alps. For this purpose, we were issued with emergency rations, very rockets, trilling whistles and, in fact, everything that might be required in the event of an emergency landing in the mountains.

The competitions began in the best of weather. The sun burned down from a deep blue sky, warming the foothills and the lower slopes of the mountains, while the up-currents were made visible to us by the delicate veils which were forming over the highest peaks and ridges into little white balls of cloud. There was practically no wind and conditions were thus ideal for our first flight into the mountains.

My turn to take off from the airfield at Salzburg came at about ten in the morning. Competitors had to cast off the tow at 1,500 feet and as soon as I had done so, I headed along the eastern slopes of the Untersberg as the side which would have caught most warmth from the sun.

At first, I encountered nothing but down-wind and I kept the airfield in view so that, if need be, I could glide down to land. I was just about to turn back when I noticed the plane begin to quiver slightly, the Rate-of-Climb Indicator rising a fraction over zero to between four and eight inches a second. Circling so as not to lose the slight up-current, I then began to climb faster, 1½ feet, 3 feet, 4½ feet per second. Above me, a cloud was forming rapidly, seeming, as it extended, to draw me up towards it. I circled higher and higher until, at about 6,000 feet, I reached the lower edge of the cloud.

The Untersberg now lay below me and, seeing a cloud beginning to form at its western edge, I flew along the ridge towards it. None of the other competitors who had started before me was visible and I assumed that they had returned to the airfield at Salzburg. It was still comparatively early and, the up-currents being weak and difficult to find, I was quite content to feel my way forward above the peaks, circling beneath small shreds of cloud and having a good look round.

The Alps, as seen from above, were new to me and the sight was indeed different from the fixed panorama of peaks to which the mountaineer is accustomed. To the airman, they seem to be in continual movement, alternately inviting and menacing as they open up, then close in again as the contrast of light and shadow shifts across them. At times, they seem even to change places with one another.

From 6,000 feet, I could see deep into the mountains. In the distance, the Grossglockner and the Grossvenediger were shimmering amid the eternal snow, while the valleys beneath me lay steaming, the mists smeared across their wooded slopes. To the South, ahead of me, the snow-capped peak of the Watzmann glittered in lonely beauty and eastwards, the Königssee, like an emerald cushioned in silken mist.

Meanwhile, above the Watzmann, a large, inviting cloud was forming. Could I reach the up-currents beneath it? I flew towards it along the ridge of the Lattengebirge, but hardly had I left the ridge, when I once more struck a down-wind. I started to fall, 12, 15, 18 feet per second and, in my concern, felt tempted to explore to right and left in search of buoyancy. But I knew that there was only one thing to do: aim straight for the nearest peak.

My proud altitude had been quickly lost and I was already under three thousand feet. The Königssee with the surrounding woods and villages came up to meet me: now I was on a level with the tree-line at the foot of the Watzmann. This was the crucial moment. Should I give up and try to land on a meadow somewhere? Suddenly, the plane lifted, gently, at first, then faster and faster. I went on rising steeply in tight turns, clinging so close to the mountain slope that my wings almost brushed the trees. We were saved—and my bird seemed to rejoice with me. I soared on in the same up-current which widened out as I gained height so that I could describe a larger circumference. The plane sailed close past the hut near the peak of the Watzmann and I could see figures waving up at the noiseless bird as, borne on the invisible air, it soared away, dwindling into the lonely spaces. Must they not have found it a strange and moving sight——?

Now I am level with the peak of the Watzmann and continue circling higher. The cloud-base stretches along the mountain ridge. 8,300 feet—8,400—8,700—9,000 feet! Now the first cloud wisps are curling round me. But the up-current is losing strength—the cloud is not going to draw me to its centre.

I have time to look round. The Watzmann gleams and shines below me. From here, though it is no longer visible, I could easily head North and glide right down to the airfield at Salzburg. But now that the great glacier regions are beckoning, I have no thought of turning back. There is one steep obstacle yet to cross, the mountain chain called the Sea of Stone.

But hardly is the Watzmann behind me than I begin to drop fast at twelve to fifteen feet per second. The down-wind is unrelenting: every second heightens the suspense. Pride in my hard-won height collapses as I sink now below the ridge of the Sea of Stone and see the great rock faces rear up closer and closer. And still my bird goes nosing down towards those scarred and wind-grieved crags, that massy, lowering, finality of rock. Is this, then, to be the end,—a cry, a crackle of sticks?

As the fear is scorching in my throat, I see, less than thirty yards away, a pair of jackdaws hovering against the mountain-side. I fly close up to them, so close, I almost brush the wall of rock with my wing. Now, I, too, can feel the lift and very cautiously I begin to circle, like the birds, ready at any moment to sheer off in a steep turn if the wind carries me too close in. I keep my eye on them, for they are better at this than I and are already above me. I follow in their wake, noticing that the lift is stronger near the places where the clefts in the rock run vertically.

After circling laboriously for half an hour, I soared at last over the glittering, snow-capped ridge of the Sea of Stone. I had lost sight of my two friends, for now a marvellous panorama was unfolded—peak after mountain peak, mantled in snow and ice, the Hohe Tauern, the Zillertaler, the Ötztaler Alps. To the South, below me, lay the valley of the Salzach and close at hand, gleaming in awesome majesty, the Grossglockner itself.

I flew on from cloud to cloud, exploring the up-wind to its highest limits and reaching, over the peak of the Hochkönig, a height of 10,500 feet. Heading, then, for the Hohe Tauern, I glided over the Pinzgau and a small bank of cloud helped me to regain the height I had lost.

When I came out of the cloud, the altimeter showed 13,000 feet. My eyes recorded that fact, then turned to the scene below. Robed as for an eternal festival, the whole mountain world lay about me in a dazzling garment of white, studded with the jewels of the glaciers, burning with blue-green fire. All was silent, timeless and at peace and as I watched, mortality, it seemed, fell from me, all mean and fretful thoughts dissolved and suddenly I was a child again, folding my hands in wonder and weeping to see the Glory of God.

In my emotion, I had forgotten all about the competition in which I was taking part and failed, too, to notice that without gloves and in my thin, white trousers, I was freezing with cold. Now, as I awoke from my dream, I could feel my teeth chattering while my hands and feet were so painful that I had difficulty in using them.

But now that the hardest part of the flight was behind me, I was not going to be defeated by the cold. So I turned my nose to the South again, where stretched the jagged peaks and terrifying spear points of the Dolomites as though waiting to impale me. I had never dreamed that my first flight would take me as far as this and my air map did not go beyond the southern portions of the Grossglockner, but, in any case, my fingers were now too stiff to hold it.

So I flew on, taking what advantage I could of the narrow up-currents over the Dolomites. To the South-West, the blue-green streaks of the glaciers gleamed on the slopes of the Marmolata, but from sheer cold I was hardly able to appreciate their beauty. A fast-moving blanket of cloud was coming up from the South-East, threatening to cut me off from the earth. The valley of the Piave now opened before me and I began to glide down the stony course of the river-bed, flanked on either side by innumerable fields fringed with olive trees. It would be no pleasure, I felt, to attempt a landing there.

As I begin rapidly to lose height, the cloud spreads out a
wall of rain, cutting off my route to the South, and the drops
start to hammer on my wings. The valley is narrowing continually and as the river bed does not invite a landing, I turn
back and head for the village over which I have last flown.
As I approach, I see to my terror that there is not a single
stretch of grass where I can land. But among the houses, I
recognise a barrack square. Three sides are enclosed by
buildings and the fourth opens on to an adjoining football
ground.

This will have to do. I glide down and am just about to fly
over a row of poplars marking the edge of the field when I
am suddenly caught in an air pocket and thrust down below
the tops of the trees. The plane seems already lost and all I
can do is to try and save myself. I put the stick down till I
am just skimming the ground and aim for the gap between
two trees. Perhaps, at the speed I am flying, the wings of the
plane will be broken clean off by the tree trunks, leaving the
fuselage to slide along the ground by itself.

Then, with only a few yards to go, I suddenly strike an
up-gust. In a flash, I pull back the stick—the plane rears up,
brushing the tips of the poplars—then pancakes heavily, but
still intact, on to the ground—and I sit there, benumbed—
and thankful.

Some time must have elapsed before a jangle of voices and
running feet brought languid life to my brain.

They were Italian soldiers—I could not speak for cold,
could not move—but they lifted me out—then they carried
my plane to barracks, in triumph, on their shoulders.

I was in Pieve di Cadore, and Salzburg lay over a hundred
miles away, on the other side of the Alps.

## 17. First Flights for the "Luftwaffe"

THE WEEKS and months passed, the tests on the dive brakes were concluded and the festive mood of the celebration party held at the Institute in honour of my appointment as Flugkapitän evaporated as we set to work on new plans and new experiments.

The German aircraft industry had meanwhile taken up Udet's suggestion and was fitting dive brakes to military aircraft. The Luftwaffe testing station was at Rechlin and in September, 1937, Udet ordered me to report there for duty as a test-pilot. This was my first incursion into the military sphere and I little suspected that it marked the beginning of a new chapter in my life, in which I was to be increasingly involved in military flying.

Before me stretched the great airfield at Rechlin, now for some weeks to be my "home,"—a very different picture from Darmstadt-Griesheim. There the slim, silvery birds would be assembled, light as swallows or the clouds that sail across summer skies. But at Rechlin, such similes were out of place. Here there were none but military planes, bombers, Stukas and the fighters that seemed like lean arrows, straining towards their mark. To me, who would naturally feel such things more strongly than a man, Rechlin had an air of grim and purposeful menace, with its continual thunder and whine of aircraft engines.

Germany was rearming. We saw it. The world saw it. But we saw it with different eyes than the world.

We young men and women wanted peace—but a just peace, which allowed us to live. And the German people wanted it, though today the world will no longer believe it. But they were a people, occupying a small living-space with neighbours on either side, who were beginning now, after years of poverty and insecurity, to have bread again and prosperity, a people who knew that the weak are always threatened and, believing themselves to share the universal right to self-protection, therefore saw in the growing national strength an increase in their own power to maintain the peace. What country in the world would not have felt a justifiable pride in the achievement?

Thus I lived through these years, little suspecting the tragedy that was being prepared. "If you wish for peace, prepare for war"—that was how I saw it, though not in those precise words. Stukas—bombers—fighters! Guardians at the portals of Peace! And in this spirit I flew them, each time in the feeling that, through my own caution and thoroughness, the lives of those who flew after me would be protected and that, by their existence alone, they would contribute to the protection of the land that I saw beneath me as I flew: ploughland and meadowland, mountains and hills, forests and lakes—the land that, though there might be others in the world more splendid, was the only land for me—for it was my home. Was that not worth flying for?

I had never before had an opportunity to test a military machine but now, in Rechlin, I flew a wide variety of types, in fact, anything that happened to be there. My heart and soul would not have been in flying, if I had not found it a great and memorable experience.

I was here for the first time encroaching on a masculine preserve and I felt that to be entrusted with a patriotic task of such importance and responsibility was a greater honour than that conferred by any title or decoration.

That the honour did not please everyone, I was soon to discover, for among the staff at Rechlin my appointment aroused not only surprise but the strongest disapproval. This only gradually became apparent, for when I first landed at Rechlin, I was welcomed most warmly by Karl Franke, Germany's best test-pilot, whom I had already met the month before, in August, 1937, at an International Air Meeting in Zürich. But once I had started daily test-flights, I could not fail to notice in all sorts of small ways the unspoken hostility of those who held that "it was not for women to play

at soldiers" and to whom the mere fact of my presence on the
airfield was an outrage.

But, in the end, the common task triumphed even over
their prejudices, so that my association with Rechlin did not
end with my return to the Research Institute at Darmstadt,
but was resumed during the war, when I was called upon to
undertake some important series of tests for the Luftwaffe.

## 18.  Flying Indoors

THOUGH TO fly is one of Humanity's most ancient
dreams, it seems extraordinary that the problem of the
helicopter had been occupying men's thoughts for centuries
before it was finally solved. We can see, for example, from
drawings made by Leonardo da Vinci about the year 1500
that he concerned himself not only with the question of
flight in general, but also with the problems of vertical ascent,
stationary hovering and backward as well as forward movement in the air.

These questions remained in the realm of theory, however,
until, in 1937, Professor Focke of Bremen constructed the
first helicopter. Using the fuselage of an existing machine, he
fitted, instead of the normal wings, two vertically mounted
lifting-airscrews, or "rotors." These were power-driven and
while rotating could be tilted by means of cams, thereby
enabling the machine to rise vertically from the ground,
remain stationary in mid-air and fly backwards or forwards.

If one is to appreciate the  sensation which this plane
caused on its first appearance, it is necessary to remember
that to those with experience of flying, an aircraft that could
hover in mid-air without moving seemed a sheer impossibility.
How, they asked, could any machine stay up without the
"lift" imparted to it by its movement through the air? To the
pilot, surely, sufficient air-speed was as essential as life itself,

for without it, his aircraft would inevitably stall and crash to the ground?

It is no wonder, then, that Udet, as Head of the Technical Branch of the Ministry of Aviation, was profoundly disturbed and excited by this new development and, indeed, I never remember having seen him so overwrought as he was at this time.

Professor Focke's test-pilot, Rolf, had flown the prototype of the helicopter and for the further tests, Focke sent for Karl Franke from Rechlin. As I happened to be in Rechlin at the time, Franke suggested I should pilot him to Bremen in a Dornier 17, a type which he knew I was particularly fond of flying. It turned out to be yet another of those strokes of good fortune which have so often befallen me, for, on our arrival, Professor Focke immediately assumed that Franke had brought me with him as his co-pilot and welcomed me accordingly. I was, of course, brimming with joy and Franke was generous enough to accept the situation as he found it.

I prepared myself for the task of flying the helicopter by making a careful study of the technical material, including the drawings. It soon became clear to me that, both in construction and method of control, the plane was something entirely new and demanded of its pilot the abandonment of all those flying habits which become second nature and the ability to make a completely fresh start.

Franke went up first. To reduce the danger to a minimum, the helicopter had been anchored to the ground by a rope, but as it was only a few yards long, the device seemed to me to have the great disadvantage of not allowing the pilot sufficient freedom to get the feel of his plane and explore gradually its characteristics.

When it came to my turn, the helicopter was first disconnected from the rope at my request and then set in the centre of a large white circle described on the ground. There was no covering over the pilot's seat and when I looked out of the open machine, I found that by aligning the tips of the air-screws with the circumference of the circle, I could detect and adjust the smallest backward or forward movement of the plane.

I now opened the throttle slowly to increase the speed of the rotors, being careful, meanwhile, to hold the stick in the normal position. Then I opened up still more, revving the engine in bursts until at last the miracle happened and the helicopter began to rise vertically from the ground, thirty feet, sixty feet, and more, like an express elevator.

Professor Focke and his technicians standing below grew ever smaller as I continued to rise straight up, 150 feet, 250 feet, 300 feet. Then, I began gently to throttle back and the speed of ascent dwindled till I was hovering motionless in mid-air. This was intoxicating! I thought of the lark, so light and small of wing, hovering over the summer fields. Now Man had wrested from him his lovely secret, how to rise up into the sky and stand there, in the fore-court of the sun, mid-way between heaven and earth.

I took a deep breath and was once more at the throttle and the stick, flying backwards, sideways and forwards again, finishing up over the centre of the circle. Then I dropped down, almost vertically, to land on the self-same spot from which I started.

Franke was the first to seize my hand and congratulate me, saying in his generous and friendly way: "No more test-flying with you, Hanna, my reputation won't stand it!"

A few weeks later the famous American flyer, Colonel Lindberg, came on a visit to Germany. It fell to me to demonstrate the helicopter to him in Bremen and I took care to draw up for his benefit a really effective programme. Lindberg, whose simplicity of manner won all hearts wherever he went, was so impressed that he called the helicopter the most striking aeronautical development he had ever seen, a tribute which made us feel very proud.

Shortly afterwards, I was given the task of flying the helicopter to Staaken, one of the Western suburbs of Berlin, where I was to fly it before a representative group of Army generals. The flight was carried out in stages, each of them setting up a new world record for this type of plane.

Meanwhile, news of the wonder-machine had spread to

Army circles and the day of the demonstration was awaited with a mixture of scepticism and tense expectation.

But, as I was soon to learn, it was not to be a Celebrity Concert: there was to be another performer on the stage, Ernst Udet in his Fieseler Storch. For Udet, greatly interested as he was in the helicopter and responsible for the forthcoming demonstration, had felt averse to this new form of flight from the start and, indeed, could never be persuaded at any time to fly the helicopter himself. And so, having been the first to show off the Fieseler Storch to the public at Zürich in the previous year, he had decided—in typically boyish mood—to enter it in unofficial competition against the helicopter.

On the day of the demonstration, there was thick fog with visibility down to less than fifty yards. To demonstrate any normal aircraft, requiring thousands of feet in which to manoeuvre, would have been impossible, but fifty yards was ample space in which to put the helicopter through its paces and so I declared myself willing to fly. Thereupon, Udet announced his intention to fulfil his part of the programme and fly the Fieseler Storch!

He climbed into his machine, opened up the throttle and, after a short run, took off—to head straight for the control building, lying hidden behind a blanket of fog about eighty yards away. The spectators took a deep breath, expecting to hear at any moment the crash of the impact, but the hum of his engine continued without interruption, fading rapidly away in the fog, and we guessed that, masterly flyer that he was, Udet had succeeded in lifting his plane almost vertically up the side of the building.

Then I took off in the helicopter, rose to fifteen feet, hovered a while so that the Generals could take a good look at me, then dropped down beside them, bobbed the machine in a curtsey, rose up vertically again, this time to stay poised above their heads, then, always at the same height as though on a dance floor, flew backwards, sideways, and every imaginable figure, dropping vertically again to a thistle-down landing directly in front of them.

They applauded vigorously and as the Chief of the Army General Staff and other high-ranking officers were also present, I received in recognition of this event and of my previous test-flying, the Military Flying Medal—the first woman ever to do so.

Meanwhile, some foreign newspapers had sought to discredit the stories about the Focke helicopter and Udet was anxious to find some means of establishing the truth of the claim that Germany was the first country to have found the solution to this centuries-old problem.

An annual spring-time event in Berlin was the International Automobile Exhibition, held in the stadium of the Deutschlandhalle. Lasting for three weeks, it was attended by a large number of foreign visitors and each evening during its course a variety entertainment was given in the stadium as a special attraction. As part of this programme, Udet now conceived the idea of flying the helicopter inside the Deutschlandhalle, so proving before an international audience that this type of aircraft had, indeed, become a reality.

The first step was to determine whether the proposed flight could be carried out without undue risk and Udet called upon me to make the necessary experiments. If these were successful, the plane was to be flown by myself as a first-night attraction and then, for the remainder of the three weeks, by another pilot.

My co-pilot and I tested together the behaviour of the helicopter inside the Deutschlandhalle and it soon became clear that Udet's plan was quite feasible. At the same time, the methods adopted by my partner and by myself were somewhat different.

To my mind, the effectiveness of the demonstration from the spectators' point of view would depend on whether the plane flew above or below them,—and if below, then to many, no doubt, the machine would appear never to have left the ground. I therefore flew as close to the roof as I could.

My partner, on the other hand, thought this was too dangerous and decided on principle not to fly more than a

few yards above the ground. My own attitude was as follows:
I was absolutely certain of my ability to fly the plane and
therefore the only possible source of danger was the helicopter
itself. If it was technically unsafe, then the height at which it
was flown was immaterial—the risk to thousands of spectators' lives ought not to be taken at all. The technical aspect,
however, was not my responsibility, as pilot, but the designer's.

After we had been training on these lines for some days,
we were surprised, one Sunday morning, to find the front
seats of the stadium filled with Luftwaffe Generals. My
co-pilot went up first, keeping, as usual, within twenty feet
of the ground. But at this height, the air currents set up by
the blades of the rotors were reflected off the ground in turbulent eddies, causing the plane to rock in an apparently
dangerous manner. This, added to the failure of one of the
steel rotor-braces on my partner's second flight, caused
Göring, rightly or wrongly, to permit the public demonstration of the helicopter to take place only on condition that
throughout the three weeks' period I myself flew the plane
at every performance.

I must admit that the prospect appalled me. Firstly, I was
to become a variety artiste! Every day during February, 1938,
at every street-corner, it seemed, in Berlin, I came upon a vast,
garishly coloured poster bearing in giant letters the word:
KISUAHELI!—and underneath: "Deutschlandhalle—Kisuaheli
—Through the Tropics at 200 Miles-per-Hour!" Then there
was a list of attractions: Dancing Girls, Fakirs, Clowns,
Blackamoors, and, "Last Item—HANNA REITSCH WILL FLY
THE HELICOPTER."

When my flying friends heard of this, they were frankly
scandalised, while my opponents, I imagined, would give a
superior smile, confidently asserting that I would next be
heard of in a night-club cabaret. But it was not for cheap
notoriety that I had agreed, with the consent of my parents,
to fly the helicopter in this strange setting, but because I
realised that the reputation of German technical skill was at
stake.

As for the setting, it turned out to be even stranger than I

had expected. During rehearsals, the technicians would be
perched on their ladders against the helicopter, calculating
with their slide-rules the correct angle of tilt for the rotors,
while all around them in the arena of the Deutschlandhalle, a
colourful throng of Circus folk practiced their turns—skinny
gymnasts with tennis-ball biceps scaling ropes or twirling
on the parallel bars, scantily clad chorus girls, stamping their
legs with energetic precision and a clown, who every now
and then would come toddling up, double-somersault,
and toddle on.

Most intriguing of all were the negroes—a novelty in
Germany before 1945. If they were not watching us at work,
they liked to sit round the helicopter reading the newspaper,
for most of them had been born in a circus troupe and knew
less, even, about the jungle than I!

As the opening night approached, tension steadily mounted and though I tried to remain calm and detached and
avoid succumbing to "footlight-fever," everything seemed to
conspire to fray my nerves. There were the posters, for
example. Try as I might to get back to my hotel after
rehearsals without seeing one, sooner or later, through the
window of my car, I would be bound to glimpse that horrid
word: KISUAHELI!

Then, there were my friends and fellow-airmen, who
somehow found their way to me, full of strident and reproachful oratory. There was my brother in the Navy, who never
ceased to beseech and implore me to withdraw from the
show. Finally, a complication was added to the performance
itself. At the end, I was told to take leave of the public with a
Nazi salute, perfectly timed and perfectly executed. I
rehearsed this in front of Udet, comfortably ensconced in an
armchair smoking a cigar, and I had plenty of opportunity
to realise, before he was finally satisfied, that flying the helicopter in the Deutschlandhalle was not, as I had imagined,
the hardest thing in the world.

The first night arrived and I found myself sitting beside
Udet in his box in the Deutschlandhalle, watching the first
half of the show. Officially, smoking was strictly forbidden,

but Udet was nervously lighting one cigarette after another,
turning to me between whiles to ask me again and again how
I felt. After a while, I could stand it no longer and during the
first interval I slipped unnoticed out of the box and watched
the performance from another part of the stadium. .

At last, at about half-past eleven, the time came for me to
get ready.

The theme of the programme was Germany's lost colonies,
at that time a much ventilated grievance, and the stadium
had been furnished with palm trees, a negro village and
other exotic paraphernalia to give the public the illusion of
an African landscape.

Into this setting my demonstration with the helicopter had
been ingeniously fitted. The plane itself was housed, out of
sight, in a native tent. At the end of the Variety Programme
proper, there was a complete black-out for a few seconds,
then giant searchlights picked out the tent as it slowly
opened to reveal the helicopter, which was then pushed into
the arena by mechanics in spotless white overalls.

There was an atmosphere of almost solemn tension among
the spectators, as if they were expecting some great sensation.
The word "Deutschland" stood, clear and beautiful, on the
silver fuselage of the plane and as my eyes read the inscrip-
tion, my heart lifted in greeting to my country, before I
climbed into the cockpit and make ready for my first
flight.

Meanwhile, a technical and historical introduction to the
helicopter was being given over the loudspeakers. At the end,
the public was instructed to hold securely on to hats and
other light articles, as a potential source of danger both to the
plane and to themselves and as I took off, the effect of
thousands of people on the floor and at the sides of the arena,
all staring up at me and clutching grimly on to some object
or other was distinctly comic.

But my attention was soon claimed by the engine of the
helicopter, which was somehow lacking in power. At first, I
could find no explanation and it was only after the phenomenon had repeated itself on the second evening that a

possible reason occurred to me—part of the oxygen required by the engine was being used up by the vast audience in the stadium.

Though the technicians at first derided this explanation, it proved to be correct and thereafter, every evening before the flight, I had all entrance doors opened wide to replenish the oxygen in the atmosphere. Only by this means could I ensure the necessary reserve of power to overcome the slight air-pockets that were continually present over the arena.

At first, the audience followed the flight intently, but very soon their enthusiasm began to wane until, at the end of the performance, there was only moderate applause.

The good Berliners were disappointed, for, to their mind, I owed them the sensation that had been promised in the programme—"Through the Tropics at 200 Miles-per-Hour" —and instead of that, the plane had risen slowly up, stood still in the air, and, slow as ever, moved sideways, backwards and forwards, then flopped leisurely to earth again.

"*Det sollen dreihundert Sachen sin?*" they murmured— "And they call that two 'undred what' names?"

"Anybody could do *that!* She don' know 'ow to fly wotcha call *fa-arst*—why don' she give us some o' the *real* stuff?"

Not only the Berliners were disappointed. Udet had expected thunderous applause but now was forced to realise that he had grossly overestimated the capacity of the general public to appreciate a purely technical achievement.

The enthusiasm and interest aroused in the aeronautical and technical world, on the other hand, were immediate and there, both the difficulties of flying the helicopter indoors and the significance of this new type of plane were fully appreciated.

But as for me, I cared little how that first performance had been received, for as soon as it was over, I longed only to get back to my hotel and be alone.

The next morning, I went to the hair-dresser. The woman behind the counter took a good look at me, then:

"Ach, Fräuleinchen," she said, in tones of friendly con-

fidence, "but I know you from last night, don't I? You was
in the show, wasn't you?"

I was . . .

This kind of thing repeated itself wherever I went. In the
street, my arm was suddenly gripped by an odd-looking
female.

"You're Hanna Reitsch, aren't you?" came an energetic
voice. "We're colleagues," she continued, "sisters, you might
say! I'm working in the same show as you—I seen your act—
that what you're doing there on the high wire with the
twirly-twizzle (helicopter!), I done something very similar
to that three years ago with the bicycle, you know—I'm
same profession as you, equilibriste and artiste-on-the-high-
wires."

I could find no reply, so she burbled on:

"You know the Machowskan—comes just before your
number?"

I thought hard for a moment and then ventured:

"You mean that sort of strange fakir-woman?"

She nodded, swelling with pride: "—My cousin!"

The performances in the Deutschlandhalle continued and
gradually, as the days passed, the enthusiasm of the tech-
nically-minded took hold of the general public, but exactly
how deep an impression my flight with the helicopter had
made on the world at large, I was not to realise till many
years later, in 1945, I came across an American soldiers'
magazine issued to the Occupation troops. The first thing
that caught my eye was my name and then I saw that it contained an article describing in popular terms my flight with
the helicopter. And as I began to read, I thought of Udet,
to whom Germany owed this and so much else beside.

## 19.  A Visit to the U.S.A.

IN AUGUST, 1938, Udet was to take part in the International Air Races in Cleveland, Ohio, but, being unable to attend, he suggested to his American friends that I should go in his stead. Two other Germans took part beside myself, Graf Hagenburg and Emil Kropf.

"We're off to see America," I remembered hearing once some street-children sing and there it was before me—the water-front of Manhattan, the Statue of Liberty, the wall of sky-scrapers—that spectacle, so many times described, whose first sight never fails to thrill, amaze and stir the heart of every European.

As soon as the ship tied up, I found myself carried helpless hither and thither in a milling throng of people, passengers, police, officials, porters and dockers, some trying to leave the ship, others pressing to come on board, zestfully impatient to greet their friends. Questions were flung at me in the strange language and, replying as best I could, I added my halting English to the babel of tongues around me. Thousands of new impressions jostled for entry to my mind, pushing and elbowing in a random, kaleidoscopic flood.

As I lay on my hotel bed—on the how-many-what'th floor?—and recovered from the exhaustion of my arrival, a phrase I had heard the porters bawling at one another kept running through my head—"What a hell goes on here? What a hell goes on?" I liked it; colourful, yet not vulgar, a phrase, I thought, that the dockers in Hamburg and Bremen would do well to study . . .

We spent a week in New York, too short a time to take in even a fraction of that vast city, to do more than gape at its immensity. Skyscrapers three hundred yards high! That was the height I had flown for my pilot's certificate—quite high enough for an inexperienced pilot. But a wall 300 yards high!

When I stood at the bottom and looked up, my eyes searching for the topmost stone, I seemed suddenly to become
smaller, to shrink away to mushroom size, almost to nothing.
And though it thrilled you, this city out of Jules Verne, ruthlessly functional like a mechanical brain, severe and purposeful in its stupendous vistas of naked concrete and steel, yet,
at the same time, you felt oppressed by it, as if weighed down
by some imponderable slab of stone.

But New York could be beautiful, too. At night, before
going to bed, when the last visitors had taken their leave,
I would go up in the lift to the roof of my hotel. From there,
the whole of New York lay stretched beneath my feet, carpeted
with myriads of shimmering, pulsing lights with, here and
there, silhouetted against them, the dark sentinel mass of a
skyscraper, unreal as shadows in some landscape of the
moon.

On all sides the glittering lights extended to where, far
away, the blue night sky bowed down to the rim of the world.
And there, beyond reach of the city's restless brain and the
traffic's noise, as it rumbled, reverberating through cavernous
concrete grooves, rose up, magnificent, God's canopy of stars.
That, I thought, must be where the open plains begin, where
the Hudson traces its silver course along green banks and
through shadowy woods heavy in mystery, where Spring
still comes to dance among the trees and where, when
Autumn's here, it rains pure gold,—there, where now the
Earth lies sleeping in the arms of Night.

Such was the potent spell that, each night, the city laid
upon its visitors and yet, like most Europeans going for the
first time to America, I had imagined I knew what to expect.
Had I not read a hundred times over, in newspapers,
magazines and books, that, though the country is the Mecca
of the Machine Age, it has neither a soul nor a mind and
hence is devoid of culture of any kind? Life in America is
business and business is money,—so we are told and so
thought all my German friends. The news that I was going
to America left them sincerely horrified. My mother shared
their feelings. "I could almost bring myself," she wrote, "to

pray God that no ship may be prepared to take your aeroplane on board."

Only Udet thought otherwise, for he knew America and with his humour, spontaneity and marked publicity sense, felt thoroughly at home there—and so, he thought, would I.

Udet was right. From the very first day, America drew me irresistibly, like a magnet, this land of easy informality that bore so many traces of the older Europe and yet, in every aspect of its life, was so entirely new and different from all that I had known.

This was brought home to me when, during the first few days in America, a great reception was given in our honour in New York. It was held in a hall of which the size alone exceeded that of any similar building I had ever seen. We were greeted by a large crowd with enthusiastic applause. Illuminated banners bade us welcome, a band started to play, and then there were a great many speeches, in which, though we could only partly understand the sense, the speakers clearly referred to us in the friendliest of terms.

When our turn came to reply, my two companions urged me to step forward on the grounds that I spoke the best English. I had no alternative but to comply, though my knowledge of the language was, in fact, so grotesquely inadequate that the mere thought of it made me burst out laughing. Thereupon, the audience started to laugh and soon, for no particular reason, the whole hall seemed to be ringing with mirth. In this jovial atmosphere, I made my speech. I was certainly neither profound, nor witty, nor even grammatically correct, but I said what I felt. I liked America, I liked it very much—so much, indeed, that, after only a few hours on American soil, I was beginning to wonder—and suddenly the phrase was on my lips—"what a hell goes on in future then?"

The effect was indescribable!

A great roar of laughter and applause broke over me, seeming never to end. Amid this thunderous outburst, I stood, dazedly wondering what I had said that was so funny and after a while, as the laughter persisted, beginning to feel

slightly embarrassed. But embarrassment seemed to be a
purely European emotion and here quite out of place, so I
chose, instead, to join in, still wondering as I laughed, why
everyone was so amused . . .

When I returned to my seat, they told me. "What a hell
goes on" was considered to be an extremely common
expression, quite unfit for a lady to use!

But no one seemed to hold it against me, on the contrary,
it brought me unexpected popularity. The next day, the
newspapers told the story in heavy print and wherever I
went, people greeted me with a smile and the enthusiastic
question: "Oh, so you are the lady who . . .?" For the
American possesses in full measure what the German so often
lacks—a sense of humour. Anyone who has caught an early
morning omnibus in New York will recognise this picture:
young and old, workers, clerks, technicians, business men,
all are buried, invisible, behind a continuous wall of news-
print. Suddenly, one of its sections begins to quiver, while
from behind it comes a crescendo of chuckles. Then the next
section begins to wobble in sympathy, till, by the time you
reach your destination, the laugh seems to have gone right
round the bus to where it started from. I could fully believe
it, when somebody told me later that, when reading his
morning paper, no American, no matter who he is, would
ever dream of missing the comic page.

Udet was right—I liked America and there was much in
the American way of living that seemed to me worthy of
imitation and I wished I could have taken back with me to
Germany. In America, for instance, the husband carries his
wife's shopping-bag and when they take the baby out, it is he
who pushes the pram. At home, he helps with the washing-
up. This is a conception far removed from the ideal of
chivalry common to most German men, but though it may
not be through churlishness that they fail to help wash-up,
neither, let is be said, does it make them twice the men to
leave it all to their wives!

In America, it is the female sex that most loudly asserts
its rights, yet nowhere have I seen women so well dressed or

so skilled in showing themselves to good advantage. They were a positive delight to the eye. The American men I liked for their spontaneous chivalry and for their lack of aggressive self-assertion. The relationship between the sexes in America seemed to me one of the most important characteristics of the country.

At my own wish, I flew from Chicago to Washington as an ordinary passenger without any of the official ceremony which normally accompanied us as guests of the country. I was anxious to see what it was like. I seated myself in the last row so that I could see the other passengers. The plane had hardly left the ground when an extremely pleasant and attractive-looking stewardess brought round papers and magazines, asked us if we were comfortable, answered our questions and was generally attentive to our wants. But although she was friendly to all, there was just sufficient remoteness in her manner to exclude familiarities.

Opposite me, on the other side of the gangway, sat a man, evidently travelling alone. The stewardess seemed to have made a strong impression on him for, on one excuse or another, he managed to claim her attentions at noticeably frequent intervals. She served him with unvarying courtesy until the moment—we had hardly been ten minutes in the air—when, unable further to restrain himself, he gave her an amicable slap. The reaction was immediate. Without a word, she turned and disappeared into the pilots' cabin. A moment later, the aircraft also turned, through 180 degrees, and started to fly back. The other passengers were just beginning to look perplexed when we touched down on the airfield. As soon as the plane came to a stop, one of the pilots appeared in front of the man and said something to him in a low voice. Whereupon, hot with embarrassment, the man got up from his seat—his bags were already on the tarmac—and walked out of the plane. Then we took off once more and continued our journey to Washington.

It was all over before most of the passengers realised what had happened and, though a more drastic way of dealing with such a discourtesy could scarcely be imagined, the

situation had been handled with such economy of emotion
that the stewardess was spared all embarrassment before the
other passengers.

Am I over-praising America?

The Head of the American Airlines offered to show me
round the airport at Chicago. My first impression was one of
disappointment. Apart from the aircraft hangars clustered
round the fringe of the airfield and a very modest looking
administrative building, there was nothing to indicate that
this was a world air-terminal and it would certainly stand no
comparison with the grandiose conception of the Tempelhof
Airport in Berlin, as I had seen it from the plans. Tempelhof
would be on a scale worthy of a great city—Chicago ought
to have been, but wasn't. This trite conclusion filled me with
arrogant and, as it proved, quite unjustified disdain.

In this mood, I followed my companion into the adminis-
tration building. Here the whole customer service was carried
out, from the prospective passenger's first tentative enquiry
to the final completion of his air-ticket. The system included
the most up-to-date ideas on organising technique. Every
word spoken during the day both by customers and officials
was recorded by invisible machines. When the day's work
was over, every employee of the airline was required to play
back at least a part of the recording, thereby getting an
objective impression of his manner of dealing with customers
which would enable him to correct, as need might be, any
faults of impatience, discourtesy or failure to supply full and
accurate information.

My mood changed to one of unqualified admiration. I
imagined myself standing in the enquiry office of some
German airline, asking for information. I imagined myself
looking at a sour-faced official, receiving his grudging answer
and leaving with the feeling that I committed some unmen-
tionable offence. In Chicago such experiences were unknown.
Here there were no impatient answers, even to the silliest
questions, no thin-lipped, dyspeptic-looking officials, no
misleading or inaccurate information. Here everything and
everybody had only one purpose—to help the customer.

"But," a German voice may object, "all this show of good manners and willingness, it is for the sake of business, that's all. It is not genuine—it is just dollar-serving deference . . ."

Does the motive matter? You do not have to love someone to be courteous to them, though Germans may think you do, and in any case, who would not prefer a mask of good manners to the most genuinely disgruntled of faces?

I went by Pullman to Cleveland, where the Air Races were to take place. Accustomed to the modest amenities of the continental railways, I was greatly impressed by the luxurious arm-chairs, the spotlessly clean sleeping-cars, the spacious cloak-rooms and the excellently efficient service in the Pullman. Here was yet another sphere of American life which seemed to function with well-nigh mathematical precision.

Certainly, the highly developed material civilisation of America has profoundly influenced its people and the European, intellectually overburdened with a centuries old cultural legacy, is often surprised by the Americans' lack of concern with problems of abstract thought. But to expect to find Faust in America would be futile. The American has other problems, the problems that a young nation has created for itself out of the superabundance of its energy in subduing a vast and virgin continent to its will. Europeans tend to judge the world by its reflection in the mirror of their own constantly critical minds, where they assess, compare and analyse their experiences till often no more than the husk remains. In normal times, therefore, when neither Continent is suffering from the after-effects of war, it should be much more pleasant to visit America than Europe, for the stranger is welcomed in America without prejudice or preconceived ideas, whereas in Europe he finds himself confronted with suspended judgement and critical reserve.

On the other hand, the American's uncomplicated acceptance of life as it comes exposes him to the danger of absorbing uncritically the opinions served up to him by Press and Radio, so acquiring a false scale of values and a uniformity of mind amazing to Europeans.

During the Air Races in Cleveland, the flags of all the
Nations taking part were hoisted each morning by beauty
queens in bathing costume—an almost sacriligious procedure
to the German mind. But Americans—to whom the hoisting
of the Stars and Stripes was a no less solemn moment—
evidently considered a beautiful woman to be the most fitting
symbol of their national values, as she, no less than America,
had been singled out by Nature for especial favour. Here,
too, the unconcerned spontaneity of the American character
showed itself. It has its dangers and it may, when he has got
to know it better, strike the European as a somewhat
inadequate response to life, but in many situations, none the
less, its effect on him is that of a welcome and beneficial
release from his own too rigid habits of thought.

Graf Hagenburg, who was an excellent aerobatic flyer,
had taken part in previous International Air Races. On this
occasion, while flying his machine on its back at low level,
he struck an air-pocket, the machine brushed the ground and
then, rending with the impact, somersaulted over and
crashed. Splinters flew in all directions and a great cloud of
dust rose up to reveal, when it subsided, a pathetic, silent
heap of wreckage. The music broke off abruptly, flags were
lowered to half-mast and the spectators rose en masse,
bearing their heads and standing to attention as "Deutschland über Alles" was played. Then, to their amazement
from amid the shattered fragments of his plane stepped—
Graf Hagenburg!

Though injured, he had himself patched up on the spot,
called for another plane and continued his aerobatics as if
nothing had happened. Nothing could have aroused more
admiration and enthusiasm among the American onlookers.
Graf Hagenburg became immediately the most popular
personality of the Air Races and remained so, unchallenged
and unrivalled, throughout the remainder of their
course.

But the German Government thought otherwise. Un-
moved alike by the enthusiasm of the Americans and the
popularity of its representative, it saw fit to recall him at

once. He had crashed, therefore he had failed—that was all there was to be said.

Before the war the International Air Races in Cleveland were held every three years and were looked upon by the Americans as an event of the first importance. Press and radio started their propaganda campaign well in advance and left nothing undone to make it effective. I, too, was called upon to make my contribution and, together with Cliff Henderson, the chief organiser of the Air Races, spoke to Rotary Club meetings in a number of towns. Generally I met with an enthusiastic response but in some places I encountered strong anti-German feeling.

The shadows of the world conflict were already sinking. I saw them here for the first time without realising that they meant war, for my thoughts belonged to the wind, the clouds and the stars, where the game of political intrigue is unknown.

The Air Races lasted three days and were attended by upwards of a million people. A variety of popular entertainments kept them amused during the intervals between events, but the main attraction was, of course, the air displays, which, in true American fashion, were designed to achieve the maximum of sensational effect.

Each day, the huge airfield was filled with the continuous thunder of aircraft engines. To me the most exciting and novel event was the pin-point parachute descents, so called because the competitors had to land within the area and preferably on the "bull's-eye" of a circle traced on the ground in front of the grand-stand. As the weather happened to be stormy, many of them—partly to avoid being blown off their target and partly, no doubt, in their competitive ardour—"spilled" too soon the air from their parachutes to increase their rate of descent, with the result that the first man to land within the circle was killed and several others had broken bones or more or less serious internal injuries.

I myself was to give a gliding demonstration in the "Habicht," the first sail-plane capable of performing all

normal aerobatic manoeuvres and constructed by Hans
Jacobs. All aircraft engines had to be switched off for the
duration of the event, so as not to mar its effect, and though
I had great difficulty in persuading the organisers of the
necessity of this stipulation and it was extremely difficult to
put into effect in view of the large number of aircraft present
and their wide dispersal, in the result a complete silence was
achieved, thanks, principally, to the help of my American
fellow glider-pilots.

After several hours of events of which the effectiveness
was held to be in direct proportion to the amount of accom-
panying noise, no greater contrast could be imagined than
the soundless swoop of that slender, shimmering bird,
gliding down like the true dove of peace rather than the
hawk, after which it was named. I performed every imaginable aerobatic figure, landing finally within the target area
of the circle amid frenzied applause.

After the Air Races were over, I received a pile of invitations from citizens all over the country, but my experience of
the great American hospitality was destined—much to my
disappointment—to be confined to this first tantalising
prelude, for one day, amid disturbing news from Czecho-
slovakia, a telegram arrived recalling us to Germany.

## 20.  Adventures in Africa

AFRICA! BLINDING sun and scorching sand; the lonely
camel, plodding patiently across the furnace of the
desert; gold-skinned, sinewy Arabs, striding grave-faced
beside their animals, their glance sharp, sometimes, as the
flash of knives, at others, baleful as the desert sky, sickening
to sulphurous yellow before the storm . . .

Though the desert still lay before us and Tripoli, where we
landed, was barely on the fringe, its hot breath already filled

the days, congealing at night to a bitter cold. Meanwhile, this was an African town and here the familiar word acquired for us a new and mysterious meaning: Tripoli, with its white houses heaped about it like irregular cubes of rock, its humanity-infested alleys, its naked, bronze-skinned children and shyly furtive women, shrouded to the eyes in the ample folds of their woollen garments, its men, crouched on the ground to trade, philosophise or ruminate in silence, while, beyond the town, on the shore in front of our hotel, the blue and glittering sea tossed up, unheeded, its silver-crested waves.

After Tripoli, we moved to an hotel lying some distance away from Homsk, the site of one of three buried cities in the area. Homsk is now only a village of a few dilapidated huts, with that lethargic rhythm of existence found everywhere in the East outside the vivid, seething life of the towns.

We had come, on an expedition headed by Professor Georgii, with three sail-planes and four towing aircraft, to study the thermal wind-currents in North Africa, as we had already done in South America.

On our modest landing-ground outside the village, we reassembled our gliders. Then we started our reconnaissance flights. But before making ready to fly—which we did almost every day—we were not to be done out of an early morning swim in the cool, sapphire blue of the sea. Then—the heat of the sun still being tolerable—we breakfasted at little, round, white-painted iron tables which at this time of day stood in front of the hotel.

For this expedition, each glider had been fitted with a wireless transmitter, not only as a safety precaution but also so that we could test its range and performance under tropical conditions.

As most of us had only started to learn the Morse Code during the voyage out, my skill as a radio operator was by no means perfect, but it would, at least, enable me to signal my position every half hour to the leader of the expedition so that the truck could follow me.

Sitting in my glider, I looked on the modest-looking con-

traption almost as a friend—a friend whom, in case of need,
I would use to fight a deadly enemy, the all-pervading desert,
with its silence, sand, thirst and death——

Had I not read that men dying in the desert have strange
hallucinations: see camels approaching from the horizon,
hear the call of human voices, while, amid the choking sand,
the gleam of cool, palm-shaded waters seems to beckon from
the haze——?

But such terrors of the imagination would soon dissolve
in the song of the aircraft's engine as it towed me aloft in my
glider. To me, that sound was as comforting as a human voice
or the protection of a strong right arm.

And yet, as soon as I was high enough and felt the plane
lift under a fine up-wind, I longed to cast off the tow and be
free. For some hours still, I would be able to sail on rising
streams of air until, between 10 and 11 in the morning, they
would collapse before the cool sea breeze.

So I would cast off, the towing plane would dwindle into
the blue and at last I could be alone with my bird above the
sparkling wastes of sand.

We had strict instructions to set our course along the roads
and caravan routes and not on any account to fly into the
uncharted desert, but every flight we made touched its fringe
and sailing, 45,000 feet above the earth, in my silver plane, I
was always filled with the longing to hover over those vast
and desolate spaces, where men are crushed like so many
gnats between the twin furnaces of sun and sand.

After some weeks of reconnaissance in the area between
Tripoli and Benghazi, we moved our headquarters from
Homsk to Garian, lying west of Tripoli in the direction of
Tunis.

It fell to me to fly one of the motor-aircraft to its new base.
I took off under a flawless African sky and, heading south-
ward, flew hour after hour to the engine's rhythmic drone,
above a waste of sand lying blanched and torpid in the sun.

All seemed settled in peaceful brilliance and not even the
most practiced eye could have detected a sign of danger.
Then, suddenly, it was there, that livid streak across the sky

that heralded a storm, and within a few, short minutes, the whole vault had turned to sulphurous yellow, lowering as if the Last Judgement were at hand.

Almost at the same moment, the storm swooped down, lashing the desert into a boiling sea of sand, whirling aloft great streamers to twist and billow in the air, till the deadly, suffocating grains had enveloped me and my plane, blotting out sky and earth and sea. They got into my nostrils, my ears and pricked and stung my eyes, finding a way, even, through my tight-pressed lips into my mouth.

Though ignorant of the fate that might await me on the ground, I decided I would have to try and land the plane before the engine became choked with sand. The landing-ground at Garian was, I knew, somewhere close at hand and while, howling with redoubled fury, the desert whipped up at me huge scarves of sand, the thought that I might still, perhaps, be able to reach it shone in me with a steady, comforting flame. The next moment, just as the engine expired, I sighted the airfield and, gliding down, was able to land in safety.

Next day, all was quiet and orderly again, as if nothing had been,—the motionless expanse of yellow sand, the sky decked once more in its silken canopy of blue. Only the derelict plane, its engine silted beyond hope of repair, remained as token of the vanished storm.

When the other two motor-aircraft had landed, the transporters had arrived with the gliders and our two Fords with the remaining members of the expedition, a new stage in our work began and for me a new series of adventures, for, in Africa, work and adventure seemed to go hand in hand.

Our flights took us constantly over unbroken, arid expanses that only rarely showed signs of human habitation and then, no more than a cluster of huts to mark the spot that cartographers had graced with a name. When I landed in my glider near these places, one thing only was certain: I was in for a new and unpredictable adventure.

There was the occasion, for example, when, after a flight lasting several hours, I spent a night in the tiny village of

Buerat el Sun, with its population of one woman and ten men.

I had landed near the village in my glider and had just got out of the machine when I saw a woman approaching. She seemed of middle age and was of considerable girth. As soon as she was within hearing, she began to pour out a stream of incomprehensible Italian, while her eyes surveyed me in cold, immodest appraisal. Apart from her slatternly appearance, there was an air of depravity about her that repelled me.

Then two soldiers of the Carabinieri appeared. I could see they were Southern Italians. Though they seemed to be of no more than peasant origin, their manner had a swaggering panache worthy of an emperor and in their black, scarlet-edged uniforms, so incongruous in that setting, they looked as if they had stepped out of an operetta. They seemed to be on terms of easy understanding with the woman and I was already feeling far from reassured, when a party of eight Italian road-workers came into view.

After a few minutes, the woman disappeared, leaving me alone with the men. Whether I liked it or not, I would have to remain in their company for some hours and I realised that at all costs I must conceal my alarm and apprehension. As unconcernedly as I could, I attempted to explain the situation to them, filling the plentiful gaps in my Italian with French and Latin words. Naturally, I gave them to understand that the truck to fetch me was due to arrive at any moment.

Realising that I was committed, meanwhile, to their sole protection, the Carabinieri waxed more gallantly ingratiating than ever. Reluctantly, I complied with their pressing invitation to accompany them to a primitive stone hut, of which I could see three close at hand, for, after all, I could hardly stand the whole night exchanging pleasantries with them by my glider and, as I knew from experience, the nights in this country could be extremely cold. In any case, wherever I was, their own sense of chivalry would be my only protection.

The hut was divided into two rooms, the only furniture being a few chairs and a table. The tiny space which we now entered was in semi-darkness, relieved only by a single paraffin lamp. I noticed that the internal wall had a rectangular hole in it and in this aperture, to my considerable dismay, there suddenly appeared a flash of teeth and a nigger, grinning at me. I wondered how I could bring myself to spend the night in this place.

The Carabinieri insisted on me seating myself at the table and gradually their chivalrous manner took on a more intimate tone and they no longer restrained their fiery glances or the occasional word of passionate appeal. It was clear that with my scanty knowledge of their language, I would not be able to keep their thoughts to the conversational plane indefinitely.

Then, casually, an arm came to rest on the back of my chair. I pushed it away, lightly but firmly, with the smile one reserves for a stranger's pestering child. It worked, for a while, until the other soldier decided to try the same line of approach,—and likewise allowed himself to be rebuffed: this time, yes, but——? And the night had barely started . . .

To become openly hostile would, I thought, be a disastrous move, so to keep them in good temper and, if possible, to divert their thoughts, I tried telling them some funny stories. As I babbled away, laughing gaily, the very be-all of the party, my eyes were searching furtively for the hands of my wrist-watch. Noting their snail-like crawl—my mouth still hammering on without pause—I clung desperately to the thought of the truck that even now must be on its way to fetch me. But would it, I wondered, ever be able to find me in the pitch dark and in this unlikely spot?

Again, I felt an arm pressing against my back, then a face came looming up towards me. I dodged quickly away and, taken aback, the two men stood staring at me with puzzled expressions.

No, certainly, they were not vicious, but they were Southerners and here, where women were as scarce as rubies and now, presented with this unlooked-for opportunity, they could hardly be expected to belie their temperament. Only their self-respect still restrained them: all power to affect the issue was out of my hands. At this thought, my spine turned to ice.

And then, an idea sprung into my mind. I looked at their faces and I looked at their gorgeous uniforms,—and I told them, I was on my way to see Marshal Balbo. I would be meeting him the very next day. Then I praised their courtesy, their consideration, their—moderation—the Marshal would wish to be informed, I was sure—their outstanding—meritorious—would recommend and no doubt he would agree—worthy—yes, I was sure—a decoration!

I had found the word. In a flash, they were beaming with joy, anticipation and resurgent vanity. Eyes bent heavenwards and hand on heart, like visionaries they stood, stroking the as yet invisible medallion, so soon to nestle there, above their breasts. And I—? I was now the most highly to-be-respected, eminent Personage of State, the repository of their most ardent hopes!

The spell remained unbroken for the rest of the night and with the daylight, came a well-known face, framed in the open door—Otto Fuchs, the Air Commander of our expedition. Immediately, I was seeing everything with different eyes,—the little room, the Carabinieri.

They took their leave of us with voluble and exaggerated courtesy, in confident expectation of favours—alas, never to come!

The area round Garian was inhabited by none but its own sons, the Arabs—proud, silent figures, who, when I landed close by them on a long-distance flight, approached me respectfully with the invitation to be their guest in their nearby dwelling.

The oldest among them conducted me. His face reflected the wisdom and nobility of his race and thousands of years of desert life seemed to have been written into it. But beneath the surface lay a wild and panther-like audacity that both frightened me and compelled my admiration.

The small hut was made of lime and sand, the only source of light to the interior being a narrow opening in the side, about the height of a man. Coming from the brilliant daylight, I could at first see nothing, then, gradually, my surroundings revealed themselves. The hut was filled with men, sitting cross-legged on the ground and eyeing me silently.

I had to sit down beside them. A pair of narrow, distinguished looking hands, clearly those of an aged man, set up beside me with neat and skilful movements an apparatus beneath which a small fire of camel dung was lighted. Out of the darkness, a metal jug for the tea appeared, which was later drunk in the form of a sugary sweet infusion from small bowls.

At first, I felt anxious and ill-at-ease, for the faces of the men seemed sinister and oppressive and the sight of them at close quarters summoned terrifying pictures to my mind. But my fears grew less, the longer I sat with them.

Meanwhile, the solemn rule of silence had been broken and although we understood not a word of each other's language, a conversation began in the form of speech and counter-speech, supported by signs and gestures and interrupted at intervals by a pause for reflection. Throughout, the Arabs' faces remained inscrutable. But they never seemed at a loss when I asked a question which no one understood, never seemed bored, never wavered from the ceremonial which the hour required.

The Arabs are famous for their patience and their unfathomable reserve, but it was something more than those qualities which I experienced that day: it was the Sacredness of Hospitality, universal and absolute, and my hosts would rather have died than abuse it.

When I realised this, I felt ashamed of my fears.

Outside the walls of Garian, the stranger came upon a curious sight. As far as the eye could reach, stretched a series of corrugations in the earth's surface shaped like mediaeval ramparts, massive and so high, it was impossible to see over the top.

In this landscape, Otto Fuchs found congenial subjects to

paint and on the days when we were not flying I usually accompanied him in his search for a suitable motif. It was not so much the ramparts which interested me as what lay on the other side of them—it was said that people were living there in burrows in the ground.

We had been forbidden to show ourselves in such places as the Arab jealously guards his home from the eyes of strangers and we had been told to avoid unpleasant incidents. But I interpreted this as applying principally to the men, as they were more strongly resented than women in the Arab quarters of the town.

So I abandoned Otto Fuchs, who had eyes only for his art, and climbed one of the ramparts. Below me lay a shaft, about forty feet in depth and the same in width, in the sides of which were a number of openings, looking from above like enormous rabbit holes. On the floor of the shaft, was a large, black pool and, rising from it, a pungent, indescribable smell. All was lifeless and deathly still and for a while I stood staring at the scene as if benumbed.

Then I climbed the next rampart and, in the following days, the ones beyond that—and always the same sight met my eyes: the gaping shaft, the dark tunnels in its walls and, over all, the silence of the tomb.

I had almost given up hope of seeing a sign of life when, one day, I came upon a charming scene. On the floor of the shaft, a slender, dark-skinned woman was busy grinding maize between two stones, while her naked, black-haired children frolicked and tumbled round her, as high-spirited as if their barren playground were a meadow of daisies.

The scene was strangely affecting, as though in this dark and joyless pit, there had suddenly shone a gleam from the bright days of my own childhood—to awake an answering light in me.

Cautiously, I tried to draw their attention and before long one of the children saw me. At first it looked at me wide-eyed with surprise, then it announced its discovery to the others. Immediately, the mother left her work and, without looking up, with a single sweep of her arm, shrouded herself

in her burnouse, leaving only a narrow slit for the eyes. With
distress, I realised that she was terrified. I made some
friendly gesture to reasssure her,—then quickly disappeared
behind the rampart.

The next day, I was there again. This time, I had brought
a few sweets which I threw to the children. They seized them
with ecstatic delight. I waved to them, laughing, and they
waved back, twirling their arms and grinning.

After that, I went to see them every day.

Then, one morning, there was a man with them—
obviously the master of the house. His presence seemed to
make no difference to the children and I concluded that he
had no objection to my visits.

A few days later, he was standing on top of the rampart
when I arrived, as if he had been waiting for me. I felt my
heart beat up into my throat. Medium-sized, sinewy, with
the bold, taut features typical of the Arab, he had none of the
dreamy tenderness of eye found in the women of his race.
And yet, his gaze seemed not unfriendly, so I plucked up
courage and offered him the few cigarettes which I had with
me. He took them with a word or two which I failed to
understand. Then, by signs, he conveyed that he wished to
take me to his wife and children.

We climbed down the wall, then followed the floor of the
shaft for a while until we came to a vertical opening almost
hidden behind a bush which was growing close to the wall. The
man took my hand and, drawing me after him, bent down
through the opening into the pitch-dark of a narrow tunnel.

While I chattered and laughed and stumbled along behind
him, my imagination was busy with blood and the glint of
curving steel. But the hand of my guide led me steadily on
and his steps never paused until a thread of light broke in on
the seamless dark, broadening and brightening until we were
once more in the daylight.

We had reached the next shaft.

Leaving me no time to recover from my surprise, the Arab
now led me to his wife, who was standing nearby with her
children. She covered her face with her burnouse as I

approached, but this time, I gently drew it away again, not, as I did so, without a smile of interrogation to her husband to obtain his consent.

All this, the children watched with great attention, their large, black eyes positively glowing under the conflicting emotions of shyness and curiosity. As usual, I had brought with me some bonbons and as soon as these appeared, all barriers fell away and the children were warbling and chirruping at me as though we had been friends for years.

I was now led through a narrow opening into a room that was really no more than a hollow excavated in the wall of the shaft. Here I found the indefinable animal smell which the Arab carries with him particularly disturbing and, indeed, at times, almost insupportable.

I had noticed four similar openings which meant that this Arab possessed four wives and, in that country, where it is the husband's duty to support his wives and their children out of his own resources, it was an indication of considerable wealth. But of the other three wives I saw nothing.

The "room" had a certain air of comfort about it. Though there were neither table nor chairs, the walls were covered with brightly coloured carpets and there were straw mats on the ground, presumably for sleeping on at night. Some earthenware jars standing against the walls provided surprisingly impressive decoration in these simple surroundings.

But what, above all, held my attention, now that I could see her at close quarters, was the woman's extraordinary beauty. Her dark, oval face, hung with glittering ear-rings, her slender wrists, rustling with bracelets of pure gold, she seemed indeed the embodiment of that veiled and dreaming loveliness that, as a child, I had gazed at, hot-cheeked, in pictures of the Orient, contrasted then, as now, with the fierce, warrior-like figure standing by her side.

She seemed to be happy, but I could not but find it sad that such moving beauty should be destined never to mingle in the broad and restless streams of life, but should have been born only to grow old and wither here, in this cave scooped out of the desert sand.

## 21.  My Home

THE TWO years ending in September, 1939 brought me
much good fortune in gliding and soaring contests. In
1938, I succeeded in setting up a World Long-Distance
Record for a Point-to-Point flight from Darmstadt to the
Wasserkuppe and back and, in the same year as the only
woman competitor, I won the great Soaring Contests for a
long-distance goal flight from Westerland, one of the North
Frisian Islands, lying due West of the German-Danish
border, to Breslau in Silesia. Finally, in July, 1939, I flew a
world record in a flight from Magdeburg, in the heart of
Germany, to Stettin, on the southern shores of the Baltic Sea.

And so it is appropriate that I say something in this chapter of my home life and of my mother, for hers was the decisive influence in my career and, indeed, in my whole life and
she had an equal share in all my achievements.

In our home in Hirschberg, in Silesia, we lived amidst
magnificent scenery, the town being bounded on the South
by the peaks of the Riesengebirge, five thousand feet high,
on the North, by the forest slopes of the Bober-Katzbach
range and, to East and West, by woods and hills which, with
their fields and castles and country mansions, gradually
descend into the open plains beyond. In Hirschberg I was
born and there I lived throughout my childhood and for me
the memory of that beloved town, now cut off from the rest
of Germany in the Russian Zone, shall never fade.

I have mentioned elsewhere that my father was an eye-
specialist. Apart from his work, he had a particular love of
music and not a day passed but we children would hear him
playing on the 'cello, sometimes between consultations with
his patients, at others, for a quarter of an hour before the
midday meal. On these occasions, we would wait standing
behind our chairs at the dining-table, to greet him, as he

entered the room, with a Tyrolean song. Each time then, his
face would relax into a happy smile, a sight which all of us
loved to see.

I must mention at this point the musical evenings at home,
at which quartets or trios were played. They took place
regularly once a week and were always attended by a large
number of music-lovers.

We children were now permitted to take part in these
soirées, making ourselves useful in small ways, for example,
in turning over the pages of the music or handing round tea
in the interval. The evenings bore the stamp of my parents'
personalities, for to them inner culture meant everything and
outward show, nothing. These evenings were able to release
my father in a marvellous way from the severity and restraint
which his sense of duty normally laid upon him, for in contrast to my mother, who was always gay, he was usually
quiet and serious. Over all the company would shine my
mother, kind-hearted and communicative, full of charm and
captivating warmth, concerning herself with each one of her
guests.

These evenings reflected the characteristic feature of my
home: humanity—simple and genuine, through and through
based on sound moral principles.

These principles were based, in their spiritual aspect, on
definite moral values which stamped themselves on us children at an early age. Beside respect for human dignity and
a sense of honour, they included the Fatherland. It was as
much alive for us as our own home—something to which one
was assigned in love and responsibility before God. From our
parents we learned that this was the same for all peoples and
for all men who lived in the spiritual and historical ties of
their country, whether they were Germans or Englishmen or
citizens of any nation. With a narrow nationalism, this conception had nothing whatsoever to do.

But despite this benevolence and his serious-minded
reserve, my father saw to it that our upbringing was not
lacking in strictness. Simplicity, for example, was the key-
note of our existence. Being a doctor, my father naturally

ensured that we received a wholesome and adequate diet, but he allowed no delicacies and the many patients who brought sweets for us children when they visited the house were disappointed to find my father would not allow us to accept them. To this rule he hardly ever made an exception.

We children—my elder brother, Kurt, my younger sister, Heidi, and I—were all of a lively disposition and it can be imagined therefore what good use we made of the large garden attached to our home and of its long entrance hall, along one side of which my father had some horizontal bars installed for us. Though, naturally, we were not allowed to play there during consultation hours, my brother and I often forgot this rule, until we were overtaken by father's avenging hand.

But I was very sensitive as a child and possessed an almost exaggerated pride, with the result that after receiving my well deserved punishment, I ran off into the woods, only returning at nightfall when fear, loneliness and contrition combined to drive me home. Once again, it was my mother who received me, gently, lovingly, asking no questions, telling no tales, making only the Sign of the Cross on my brow. The worst punishment of all was to see from her eyes how much she had feared for me, for that made my heart turn over with remorse.

Thus my father exercised in our family a strict and uncontested authority based on firm moral and spiritual principles, but it was my mother who made our happiness complete. I cannot remember her as other than gay and calm of spirit. Her goodness to us was unbounded, and she was very clever. As a girl, she had had an excellent education in Vienna at the Imperial Civilian Boarding School for Girls, acquiring a solid fund of learning, as well as a good knowledge of several foreign languages. To us she was untiringly patient, loving, consoling and edifying—as, in their hearts, all mothers are with their children, but hers was also the gift, not given to all, of subtly making us aware of these qualities, and thereby our lives became wonderfully enriched.

Shall I relate how, on the daily walks which she took with

us, she taught us to see the flowers, the grass, the beetles and
the birds, the sky and the clouds, or how she made the sun,
the moon and the stars a part of our childhood world? How
at the Feast of the Epiphany, she sent us in to my father's
patients, dressed as the three kings, Caspar, Melchior and
Balthazar, wearing sheets and crowns of gold paper? Whenever we played as children, she would be close at hand,
watching unobtrusively, ready to intervene when necessary
to teach us to be self-reliant and inventive.

In those early years, my upbringing must have caused her
some concern, for of her three children I was by far the most
sensitive and highly strung, confronting her with the unexpected on many occasions.

When, for example, at the age of four, I spread my arms
and tried to jump off a first-floor balcony, my mother
clutched me in terror: "Child! You'll kill yourself!" "Would
I be dead then?" I asked. "Would I be with our Father?
Would he say, 'Hanna, shall we make it hail?'" At that time,
nothing delighted me more than a good storm of hail . . .

That I chose, later, to do my home-work sitting in the topmost fork of a tree may not have met with her entire approval
but at least it caused her no undue alarm, for she knew by
then that I was strong and had a good head for heights.

My attempts, on the other hand, to outdo my brother in
the art of regurgitation seemed to her to have nothing to
recommend them and when, one day, I gave an unsolicited
demonstration of my skill at the dinner table, I was quick to
receive a box on the ears. After that, I transferred my performances to the cellar.

My mother was skilful in the art of educating her children.
Finding, for example, that I was inclined to form my likes
and dislikes by immediate impressions and was over-hasty in
my judgements, she did not simply ignore my opinions, as
adults often foolishly do when dealing with children, but left
them uncontested until, as I thought by chance, I would
discover my mistake through some illustration which she was
careful to supply.

In this connection, my mother took particularly seriously

the task of teaching me to think justly and kindly of my
fellow men and some years later I found she had written
Moltke's lines in her diary:

> "Genuine good manners and refinement are the effects
> of a friendly and benevolent disposition. Sincere modesty
> and lack of pretention are the only safeguards against the
> slights and snubs of this world. So long as we do not aspire
> to seem otherwise than we really are, neither rank nor
> birth, magnificence nor the multitude can have power to
> disconcert us."

Between my mother and myself the bond was particularly
close. Already as a child I felt this, but its peculiar strength
and intimacy I only fully realised later when, after I had left
home, she wrote to me every day during my flying career so
that her influence came to play a truly vital part in my life.
In all things, I felt her beside me and so intensively did she
live with me in imagination that when I needed her help,
though we had been separated for months, she could come
to my aid in a moment.

It happened repeatedly, even in small things. If, for
example, on some rare occasion, I had to make a speech but
had been too busy to prepare anything, I would simply go
to the telephone: "Mother, please think out for me what I
should say tonight," and tell her the few main heads of what
I wanted to talk about. Before long, in good time for the
meeting, would come the awaited reply. My mother would
tell me quickly over the telephone what she had put together.
The thoughts she suggested were always highly individual
and unusual. Yet curiously enough, I never used any of them,
for once I found myself looking into so many interested and
questioning eyes, speaking always came easily to me. But my
mother's help was invaluable, for it gave me the quietness of
mind from which I could produce my own thoughts without
difficulty. I could relate countless similar incidents.

My decision to volunteer as a suicide-pilot I discussed with
her and here, as always, she remained true to herself. For
years she had known that I was exposing my life to ever

greater dangers, yet she never complained—and, indeed, what use would it have been? I understood precisely how she felt, how each day she had to conquer her fears afresh, for she was incapable of learning to accept such a state of affairs, as some people can. Yet she controlled her anxiety with such fortitude and faith that her unshakable confidence became a kind of shield to me.

The time came when countless of those around me met their deaths in the performance of the selfsame duties as my own. But mother did not allow her faith to be shaken and it withstood the hardest tests. At the same time, her judgement remained clear and untroubled. If I was faced with a decision and asked her advice, she invariably chose the course which her conscience prescribed, though it might be the hardest and most dangerous for me to take. It cost her a bitter struggle, but that was how she was made.

One more thing I would say. Among my mother's rare qualities of heart and spirit, the greatest was the power and depth of her love. I could ask anything of her, anything in the world. When real help was needed, nothing was too difficult and her love was so strong that even the mere thought of it, even when far from home, fulfilled me with warmth and happiness. Yes, truly; so long as she was there, no evil could befall her child.

And so, ever since I left Hirschberg at the end of my schooldays, wherever I have been, the sights and sounds of my home have gone with me: the shivering rustle of the trees lining the broad road beside our house, the great peaks of the Silesian mountains, the clouds sailing across the summer skies—and then picture upon picture comes crowding back of that life, so greatly loved and so sorely missed.

## 22. Test-Pilot in Wartime

HAVING CONCLUDED our work on dive brakes at the Glider Research Institute, we now turned to the task of constructing a glider of much greater size. Our first project was to build a kind of flying observatory for obtaining meteorological data. The scheme developed into an attempt to build a freight-carrying glider, to be used, for example, by the Post Office for transporting mail. In this particular case, the glider would be towed by a mail plane and land for deliveries at places where the former did not call.

In the state of research then prevailing, the construction of such a glider was a bold undertaking, as it depended on finding solutions to various new technical problems. How, for example, was a glider designed to carry heavy loads to be towed to the required height? How would it behave on tow behind a multi-engined plane? The answers to these and many other problems could only be obtained by experiment.

I was asked to test-pilot the first prototype transport glider constructed at the Institute. Towed by a Junkers 52, I tested the glider cautiously, stage by stage. Only when I was completely satisfied with the plane's performance, did I start to fly it with a load, at first one sack of sand, then two, adding a further sack each flight until the maximum load was reached for which the glider was designed. Then, and then only, did I take my first human passenger.

After weeks and months of test, modification and further test, we were at last satisfied that the freight-carrying glider was ready to go into use as an addition to existing means of communication.

This was indeed a turning-point in the history of gliding, for in the past it had been looked on purely as a sport, its practical usefulness being a matter of conjecture. But now that we had proved it possible to design gliders for a variety of different uses with the same degree of accuracy as powered aircraft, a much wider interest began to be taken in their further development, in particular by the Wehrmacht.

Being noiseless in flight and able to dive at steep angles, the freight-carrying glider seemed to the High Command of the Army to offer an excellent means of landing bodies of infantry by surprise behind an enemy's lines, and to the strategists this opened up new and fascinating possibilities.

Accordingly, the Glider Research Institute was asked to design a troop-carrying glider. The plane was to take ten fully equipped infantrymen, plus their commander, and the minimum of materials were to be used in its construction as it was intended to be destroyed after landing. An unusual feature was the fuselage, which was to be made of steel tubes, but in other respects it was to fulfil the requirements of any normal aircraft, that is, adequate rigidity, good flying qualities, a fair safety margin and the means of giving some protection to its passengers in the event of heavy landings on rough ground.

When construction and testing had been completed, the troop-carrying glider was demonstrated before representatives of the Services. The importance which the High Command attached to the project can be judged by the fact that among the high-ranking officers who attended were Udet, Ritter von Greim, Kesselring, Model and Milch.

Although the whole affair was organised entirely by the military, I was asked to carry out the demonstration flight as I had been responsible for testing the prototype. The Generals stationed themselves on the edge of the airfield, the ten men with their commander climbed into the plane and we took off, towed by a Junkers 52. At somewhat over 3,000 feet, I cast off the towing cable, put the glider into a steep dive and landed her near some tall bushes, only a few yards from where the Generals were standing. The troops tumbled out and in a matter of seconds had taken cover and disappeared from sight.

The speed and precision of the whole manoeuvre so fired the Generals' enthusiasm that one of them suggested an immediate repetition, this time with himself and his colleagues as passengers. The idea was heartily approved by all, with one exception—myself! As for me, I nearly fainted at the thought of the truly awe-inspiring responsibility that had been thrust upon me.

But all went well and I managed to restore my precious passengers safely to earth. After the generals had warmly thanked me and walked off, beaming with pleasure, to talk over their experience, I suddenly noticed a human form prising itself out of the tail of the glider—Hans Jacobs, the designer!

The usefulness of the glider from a military point of view did not, however, remain uncontested. The chief objection came from the parachute formations who saw in it a source of unwelcome competition and, as a consequence, a wide difference of opinion developed in Army circles.

It was therefore decided that a second demonstration should be held, this time before the Army General Staff. It was arranged that ten gliders carrying infantrymen, towed by Junkers 52's, and ten Ju 52's carrying paratroops should take off together from the same airfield and fly, maintaining an equal height, to the airfield at Stendal. Not being invited to act as pilot on this occasion, I watched the planes land. For me, it was a curious feeling to see our gliders under the control of strangers and I experienced something of the same anxiety that a mother must feel when, for the first time, her children venture beyond the protection of home.

In the result, the glider-borne troops had a definite advantage. The gliders dived steeply towards the airfield, came to rest in close formation and discharged their occupants as a formed body of men. The paratroops, on the other hand, had the ill luck to encounter a stiff breeze—from which the gliders had actually benefited—and landed widely dispersed, in some cases a considerable distance from their ammunition and stores. Though this experience could not, of course, obscure the importance of paratroops in a future war, it at least proved conclusively that the troop-carrying glider could become a weapon of great value.

As soon as war broke out in 1939, a force of troop-carrying

gliders was, in fact, brought into being for a special task, namely to land troops and equipment on top of the forts in the Maginot Line during the invasion of France. The forts—according to the Operations Plan—were to be overcome as quickly as possible with the minimum number of troops, thereby enabling the main force to pass through with comparative ease.

The unit created for this purpose comprised the pick of Germany's glider-pilots, but not being professional soldiers, they were given the status of Other Ranks and the disparity between their military grading and their technical ability—reflected in reverse in those responsible for their training, who had officer rank and little knowledge of flying—was destined to have the most unfortunate effects on the manner in which they were prepared for their task.

The date originally fixed for the invasion of France was several times postponed and meanwhile the glider-pilots remained with their unit in the strictest isolation, forbidden, because of the importance of their task, to go on leave or even to write letters home. While their time was passing in inactivity, they were all too well aware that, inadequately planned and rehearsed as it was, their hazardous task nevertheless required the most thorough preparation if it was to succeed, for no similar undertaking had ever before been attempted, in peace or in war.

According to the Operations Plan, the gliders were to take off at short intervals, as they were required to land on their targets at almost the same moment. They were to be drawn up side by side on the airfield, each glider connected by a cable to its tug.

But what would happen if, in the darkness, the tow-ropes became entangled?

The Plan detailed for each glider the precise minute at which it was to land on its target and the whole subsequent operation was planned on the assumption that this time-schedule would be successfully carried out.

But how?

Knowing that the operation would tax their skill to the

utmost and having found no answer to these questions, the glider-pilots tried all they could, or all that military etiquette would allow, to impress on their officers the necessity of detailed rehearsals.

Their plea fell on deaf ears: what could mere Lance-Corporals know about the planning of military operations?

Can it be wondered that, with the knowledge that precious training time was being lost while they waited, condemned to inactivity, cut-off from their families, their friends and their flying companions, the glider-pilots became ever more demoralised, ever more embittered?

Once this situation came to my ears, the thought would not leave me that sheer ignorance and lack of preparation might cause this whole enterprise to fail and cost my comrades their lives. For days and nights on end, I tried to think of something I could do to help them. Above all, I wanted to establish contact with my friends, so that I might try to relieve their bitterness and depression. I wrote to General von Richtofen, among whose numerous commands the Glider Unit was included, asking if I might take part in the operation as a pilot. Richtofen refused. Though it now seemed impossible for me to reach my friends, I could not altogether give up hope of doing so, for so often in the past some wonderful stroke of fortune had come to help me in time of difficulty.

Meanwhile, winter had arrived, bringing frost and ice. The invasion of France, fixed for November, was postponed until February, 1940, as the former date had become known to the enemy.

For the gliders, this brought the problem of how they could be halted quickly when landing on an icy surface. There was no time for lengthy experiment and the Glider Research Institute simply received the laconic request to construct brakes suitable for the purpose.

The solution was found by Hans Jacobs, who devised brakes in the form of plough-shares, to be mounted one on either side of the landing skids and operated by moving a lever. The effectiveness of these brakes remained to be seen, as it would vary with the nature of the ground and the landing speed of the glider.

That their braking power was much greater than we had imagined, I was to discover on the very first test. To prevent the control column digging into me if the glider came to a sudden stop, I had padded myself out with a number of blankets, but when I applied the brakes, their effect was so strong that I was thrown violently forward against the safety-belt and completely winded. For some minutes I was too dazed to move and finally, white as chalk, had to be helped out of the machine. Modifications were then made to the brakes to reduce their ploughing effect. I flew test after test, at first with an empty machine and then with full load, until finally the brakes were declared satisfactory.

It was with great joy that I received, soon after, the request to demonstrate the new brakes to my friends in the Glider Unit at Hildesheim. My wish to see them was, after all, to be fulfilled and I felt sure that, by this means, their problems would be solved.

The Commanding Officer met me at the airfield at Hildesheim with much cordiality and, amid his demonstrations of goodwill, would have found it difficult to refuse my request— which I put to him as soon as I arrived—to be excused lunch in the Officers Mess and be allowed to eat, instead, in the canteen with my old flying friends. True, he could not altogether withhold a trace of displeasure from his expression but it left me unconcerned.

Naturally, at the mid-day meal I saw nothing but happy faces. But I could see that the canteen was not the place to discuss what was on all our minds. We would have to wait for a better opportunity. This occurred in the evening, after a day spent in demonstrating the new brakes to the members of the Glider Unit. A night exercise, which I had been invited by the Commandant to attend, had to be abandoned owing to fog and for a few hours I was "off duty" and free to rejoin my friends.

Gathered round a plain, barrack table in the men's quarters, we were a small group of pilots, all with long experience of gliding, headed by the splendid Otto Bräuti-gam. For the first time, I heard the whole story, in fact and detail. For the operation against the Maginot Line, hardly a single practice flight had taken place, let alone a full-scale rehearsal. We did not dispute that timed-to-the-minute landings were essential if the operation was to succeed and unnecessary loss of life to be avoided, but to achieve these, training flights would have to be undertaken at night, both short-distance and long-distance. Every possible eventuality must be anticipated and studied in advance.

Otto Bräutigam was the liveliest among us, fizzing with vitality, full of pranks and jokes, yet speaking plainly, almost harshly to the point and, with it all, a most able and coura-geous flyer. Now his face was set in bitter and deadly earnest as he spoke out against the treatment which he and his com-rades were receiving. I knew that none of them could be called a coward and that they all were ready to give their lives in battle. And they were not mere mutineers, either, kicking against a necessary system of discipline. But, surely, no military organisation could maintain a fossilised and formalistic caste system with the sole object of cloaking its own inadequacies in conducting a war or afford to accept complacently the sacrifice of human lives on the grounds that the voice of Corporal Otto Bräutigam was too insig-nificant to be heard in its affairs? It was against this that my friends rebelled and that everything in me also rose up in protest.

But where they had failed to obtain a hearing, a woman would surely have even less chance? My friends would not believe me. To them, the very fact that I was a woman and so outside the sphere of military authority was an advantage.

But what exactly could I do? It would be worse than use-less for me to try and intervene personally, for the military mind would never conceivably concede to a female the right to be heard in matters of exclusively military concern. The way out was found by Otto Bräutigam, who some days later succeeded in obtaining an interview with General von Greim.

This resulted in the holding of a large-scale rehearsal which confirmed in catastrophic manner the doubts which my comrades had held. Apart from difficulties at the take-off, only a few of the gliders ever reached their target at all and those were hours behind schedule. But at least there was still time for these matters to be put right in an adequate training programme.

The test-flights which I carried out for the Glider Operation, as, indeed, my whole work at this time, had as object the saving of human lives and for that reason alone, quite apart from my love of flying, I could not have wished for a more satisfying task.

The whole of German aeronautical research was soon to be harnessed to military needs and as a test-pilot I was increasingly to come in contact with the Services. Those officers to whom the maintenance of masculine privilege was more important than the needs of the hour were naturally put out by the fact that I was a woman. Their obstructive attitude was to cost me many battles and would often have delayed the excution of vital work had it not been for the timely help of men like Udet and Ritter von Greim, who were intent on a larger struggle than the battle of the sexes and, thanks to their rank and position, were able to smooth my path. This attitude of prejudice naturally caused me some distress at times but it could never have deflected me from doing my duty, which throughout those war years laid upon me the heaviest and most exacting toil.

It goes, perhaps, without saying, that not every test or project on which we worked was destined to bear fruit, for, in technical matters, the idea that seems brilliant on paper does not always prove feasible in practice. But even our failures serve to indicate the intensity with which German air research was pursued under the pressure of war-time necessity. In this work the Glider Research Institute was to take an increasing part.

One of our experiments about this time was the attempt to construct a flying petrol tanker, to be towed behind the parent machine as a pilotless glider, to enable the former to refuel in the air. The tanker would have to possess the greatest possible inherent stability so that it would return to a level course of its own accord after passing through atmospheric disturbance.

This meant that, though of small dimensions, it would have to be fitted with controls in the experimental stage, as only its own pilot could determine exactly its behaviour in the air. I was particularly suited to act as test-pilot on account of my small size.

In my almost ten years' experience as a test-pilot, no flights proved so great a strain as these. In order to test the limits of the glider's stability, I had to lock the controls and deliberately allow it to get into difficulties. As a result, it often turned turtle when on tow and every time I went up in it, I had to fight against the most violent onslaughts of air-sickness and often, as well, against the most primitive and hateful fear. In due course, the flying petrol tanker was proved to be impracticable in this form and the experiments were discontinued.

Further experiments were concerned with finding a way to enable small observation planes to take off and land on war-ships, using only the smallest deck-space.

For this purpose, a series of ropes, each about 100 feet long, were stretched out in an inclined plane, one end being fixed to the deck and the other, drawn over a 20 feet high wooden scaffolding. On this the aircraft was to land, the wings and elevator coming to rest on top of the ropes and the fuselage, in the 3-foot space between a pair of ropes. Each rope was fitted with a number of braking devices, intended to halt the aircraft within the available space of 100 feet.

My task was to land the aircraft securely in the ropes and so that they would not saw through the wings, a steel tube was fixed on the underside of the wing-surfaces and the elevator.

There remained the danger that, in landing, the machine would jump out of the ropes. To prevent this, a device was fitted by which the impact of the fuselage on the ropes caused the two on either side of it to spring into a rigid channel which then closed over them, so holding the aircraft steady and confining its further movement to a straight line.

For these experiments, it was intended to use a small machine with a pusher airscrew, that is, a propeller mounted behind the wings, but as the plane was then still in the experimental stage, it was decided that I should use a glider instead, with the object of testing, first, whether the principle of the idea was sound. As it turned out, my task was exceptionally difficult.

As will be realised from the details I have given, it would be necessary for me to make a spot landing with absolute precision and before making the tests, I trained for this systematically. I had a landing-ground marked out with flags on a neighbouring airfield of exactly the same size as the bed of ropes on which I was to land. Every morning before the test-flights, I practiced  precision landings at the slowest possible speed on this patch of ground.

At close quarters, it was extraordinarily difficult to see exactly where the inclined plane formed by the ropes began and to make it easier to recognise, I had some small fir-trees placed between the ropes which gave an added appearance of depth to the picture and so made recognition more simple.

All preparations having thus been made with the greatest care, I made ready, amid tense expectation, to fly the first test. Once again, I padded myself out with blankets and—at the risk of some secret smiles from the bystanders—decided, on this occasion, to wear a crash-helmet.

Though I touched down with precision on the spot intended, a slight beam wind twisted the machine at the last moment and, still moving at a good speed, in a flash the hull plunged down at an angle between two of the ropes. Instinctively, I ducked but even then it was only thanks to the crash-helmet that the ropes did not slice my head from my body.

The onlookers found this moment more terrifying than I. Some fighter-pilots who happened to be watching swore they would rather fly any number of sorties against the enemy than attempt a flight of this kind.

On the second test, I landed nicely according to plan between a pair of ropes but in spite of the braking chocks, my air speed was still considerable and it was no pleasant sight to see the 20-foot high scaffolding come rushing inexorably towards me. However, with a few yards still to go, the machine unaccountably came to a stop.

Then came the third test, this time, with a new type of braking device which completely failed to work. Again, the scaffolding at the upper end of the ropes came hurtling towards me. Again, I ducked instinctively. This time, there was no doubt about it, I was going over the edge. But the tail, by some miracle, got stuck in the scaffolding and only the front part of the fuselage, with myself inside it, went over and hung, suspended in mid-air, until they brought fire-ladders to release me.

These experiments, also, were finally abandoned, as meanwhile another and better solution had been found.

A task which I found particularly worthwhile was the experimental work in balloon-cable cutting. It will be remembered that in its operations against England, the Luftwaffe met an unforeseen obstacle in the barrage-balloons, particularly over London. They were the cause of many casualties among Luftwaffe personnel as the balloon cables, when an aircraft flew into them, cut straight through the wings.

Hans Jacobs constructed a fender to protect the engines and wings and divert the balloon cable to the wing-tips where a cutting device was installed.

The device was to be tested near Rechlin, starting with steel cables of 2.7 millimeters in diameter, then increasing in thickness till a diameter of 8.9 millimeters was reached, at which size the cables seemed to stand up in the air like steel tubes. The most delicate instruments were installed in the aircraft to measure the force of impact as it flew into the cable, thereby providing the data necessary for the further development of the fender.

I was detailed to carry out the tests in a Dornier 17 bomber. As it could not be foreseen whether, in practice, the fender would afford complete protection to the airscrew, the possibility could not be excluded that broken fragments might be hurled through the cabin and fatally injure the crew. I therefore had a second pilot's seat with duplicate controls built into the rear gun-turret, close by the escape hatch. Though the machine could not be landed from that position, it could, at least, be controlled in the air.

Before the take-off, I briefed the fitter in detail. As soon as we reached a safe height, he was to hold the aircraft steady while I climbed back to the gun-turret and took over the controls from there. He was then to join me, fasten our parachutes and, having done so, install himself near the escape hatch. If the test was a failure, we should, if we had sufficient height, be able to bale out. When my task was to fly into the balloon cable at low altitudes, there would be no question of baling out for either of us and on those occasions, therefore, I flew alone.

At length, we were ready for the first test-flight. I climbed into the Dornier 17 and, taking off from the airfield at Rechlin, climbed until I could look down on the balloon from above. Then, circling slowly, I searched round for a sight of the cable. As soon as I had located it, gleaming silver in the sunlight against a background of blue sky, I came down a little and in so doing lost sight of it again. I then flew towards it, gauging its position from memory and, sure enough, in a few moments struck it at the spot where I expected it to be.

From now on, so as to make it easier to spot the cable, I arranged to have strips of bunting several yards long attached to it at intervals of 100 feet. I would take a pair of strips as markers and aim at a point on the cable mid-way between the two.

The effectiveness of the cable-fender was by no means proved in the first few flights and could only be assured by continuous improvement of the design based on data obtained from sensitive instruments in the plane which recorded

every detail of impact and stress at the moment when the
aircraft came in contact with the cable. The diameter of the
latter was progressively increased to the thickest likely to be
encountered in operations over England.

Like few others, these experiments had laid hold of my
imagination, for every test I flew brought us a step nearer to
overcoming some of those perils which pilots and aircrews
had daily to face in operations against the enemy. Such was
my enthusiasm, I was hardly aware that for days I had not
been feeling well. Despite headache and high fever, I was
determined to go on until the last test had been completed,
for now it only remained to subject the fender to the final test
of strength by flying into the thickest cable of all. I managed
to fly several more tests until, shivering with fever, I discovered, one morning, the unmistakable symptoms of
scarlet fever.

I was sent straight to the Virchow hospital in Berlin,
where they put me in a small room in the isolation wing with
a view on to a pleasant garden. My temperature went up
and up and within a few days the rash had spread to my eyes.
That meant that the windows of my room were completely
blacked-out and I had to lie in total darkness. I wondered
what the future held for me and whether I would be able to fly
again. After a few weeks, I developed muscular rheumatism
and my heart became affected. The days were dark indeed.

Meanwhile, the tests were successfully concluded by a very
able flyer and friend of mine, Lettmaier, who was later killed
in action.

The balloon-cable fender was now ready for operational
trial, but the Luftwaffe was sceptical. An exception was
Ritter von Greim, who held the rank of General-Oberst, the
equivalent of Air Marshal. He and his senior officers had
witnessed the tests and were convinced of the value of the
device. He therefore asked for all machines that were fitted
with the fender to be transferred to his command. His pilots
were the first to write and thank me after the planes had
proved themselves in action and nothing could have made
me happier than the letters I received.

Three months had now passed and I was discharged from hospital, completely fit and able to fly again. I returned at once to my work as test-pilot.

Though the cable-fender had proved its worth, its weight would become too great for the aircraft if one engine went out of action and consequently it was to be abandoned in favour of a strip of razor-sharp steel, to be fixed to the leading edge of the wings and intended to cut any balloon cable that the aircraft might encounter. No protection was afforded, by this method, to the airscrew.

Each time we cut a balloon cable on the tests, it meant the loss of the balloon and consequently we had to transfer our experiments to the balloon-testing station at Saarow.

An unforeseen difficulty arose in that, whenever there was a stiffish breeze, the released balloons, dragging the upper end of their cable with them, caused considerable damage to the electric wires of the grid system and that, coupled with the high rate of consumption of balloons, must have cost the State a fortune. Attempts were made to shoot down the drifting balloons with fighters, or, when no fighters were available, the pressure release valves on the balloons were closed down so that, on reaching a certain height, the balloons would burst. Neither of these methods was however, entirely effective.

One day, Ernst Udet touched down at Saarow on his way to a conference with Hitler. To his amazement, he was told that I was just about to carry out one of our tests and fly into a balloon cable. He had been quite unaware that it was I who had been doing this work regularly, day after day, for weeks on end. He had never witnessed one of these tests before and stayed with the balloon crew below to watch.

On this occasion, a cable was to be used that was particularly difficult to cut. Though only 5.6 millimeters in diameter, instead of consisting of a large number of steel threads, it was made of five or six strands, each much thicker and tougher than usual. The cable had drifted over with its balloon from England but unfortunately only a short length had been found, with the consequence that, in the test, the

balloon would have to be flown much lower than usual and
the aircraft would not have sufficient height for me to bale
out in case of necessity.

The balloon cable was anchored in a wood, where there
was protection from the wind, and hence the balloon only
turned into the wind when it had passed well above tree-
level and a considerable length of the available cable had
already been paid out. When it did so, however, instead of
turning its nose into the wind, it slewed round till it was
broadside-on. This meant that the balloon would have a
much stronger drift than usual and might snap its cable at
any moment. The crew should, of course, have lowered the
balloon as soon as they saw this, but, instead, in their
anxiety, no doubt, not to disappoint their visitor, acted as if
all were normal and gave me the signal to start.

I realised, as I flew over the balloon and saw the unusual
position into which it had been driven by the wind, that to
fly at low level into so steeply slanting a cable would be
fraught with danger, but assuming, as the ground-crew had
given me the "All-Clear," that cables in this position were
encountered on Active Service, I was determined that the
test must be carried out. At that moment, the cable parted.
A split second later, the metal splinters of an airscrew shot
through the cabin and the starboard engine began to race at
high speed. The cable had shaved off the lower edge of two
propeller blades. I immediately switched off the damaged
engine and engaged the electric motor in an attempt to
"feather" the propellers, that is, to halt them in the neutral
position, where they would not continue to turn by auto-
rotation. But could I do it before the frantically racing engine
tore loose from its mountings and the aircraft, suddenly
becoming tail-heavy, inevitably crashed? It was a race
against Death.

Hearing the crack of the parting cable and seeing the air
filled with metal fragments, Udet and the men with him
watched, frozen with horror, as I disappeared out of sight
over the tree-tops, then waited for the sound of the inevitable
crash. Hearing nothing, Udet then flew in his Storch to

Fürstenwalde, from where I normally took off for the tests
and where, on this occasion, I had also successfully landed
the aircraft. I was greatly surprised when he landed close by
my machine, looking paler than I had ever seen him. He
stood; taring at me, unable to speak a word. Then, when he
had recovered from his fright, he flew on to his conference
with Hitler, to whom he described the whole incident.
Thereupon I was given the Iron Cross, Second Class.

## 23. The Iron Cross

ON 27th MARCH, 1941, Göring received me at his house
in Berlin, and in recognition of my work as test-pilot
conferred on me a special version of the Gold Medal for
Military Flying with Brilliants. Surrounded by his Generals,
Göring was standing ready to greet me when I entered the
room. At first, however, he took no notice of me, but continued to stare straight over my head in the direction of the
door.

After a few moments, Udet smilingly drew Göring's attention to the fact that the person he awaited was already
standing before him.

Göring's amazement was great. He planted his bulk
squarely in front of me, his hands resting on his hips.

"What! Is this supposed to be our famous 'Flugkapitän'?
Where's the rest of her? How can this little person manage
to fly at all?"

I did not like the reference to my size. I made a sweep with
my hand roughly corresponding to his girth.

"Do you have to look like that to fly?"

In the middle of my sentence, it suddenly struck me with
hot embarrassment that, in the circumstances, my gesture
might be considered out of place. I tried to halt it in mid-air,

but too late—everyone, including Göring, had seen it and
there was a great burst of laughter, in which Göring joined.

The following day, Hitler received me in the Reich Chancellery to confer on me the Iron Cross II. His Adjutant led
me through a long corridor to the room where Hitler, Göring
and one or two other people were assembled. This was the
second time I had been presented to Hitler, the first occasion
being in 1937, when the honorary title of "Flugkapitän"
had been conferred on me.

Hitler greeted me with friendly warmth, while Göring
stood beside him, beaming like a father permitted to intro-
duce a prettily mannered child. Then I was invited to seat
myself between them at a large, round table, on which, as I
vividly remember, there stood a vase of early sweet peas.
Hitler questioned me at length about my test flights, particularly those connected with the experiments on dive
brakes. He was also interested in the experimental work done
on the cutting of barrage-balloon cables. His knowledge of
technical aeronautics, reflected in the searching pointedness
of his questions, struck me as remarkable for a layman. At
this formal reception it was impossible to obtain any deeper
insight into Hitler's personality and character.

Since its institution in the year 1813, the Iron Cross
(Second Class) had only once before been awarded to a
woman, the nursing sister Johanna Krüger, and its confer-
ment on me, the first woman to receive it in this war, was a
source of considerable public interest and satisfaction. In the
days that followed there descended on me from all parts of
Germany a very large number of letters, telegrams and
personal congratulations.

My native province of Silesia hastened to do honour to its
child and on 4th April, 1941, a great reception was accorded
to me in my home town of Hirschberg. At first I had been
reluctant to make an appearance, but the matter was settled
in drastic fashion by the mayor, Oberbürgermeister Blasius,
who came by car to Berlin to fetch me.

Still full of the impressions of the last few days, I was

awakened to a realisation of the local enthusiasm as soon as we reached the Silesian border. The villages were decked with flags, people at the roadside threw flowers or waved to us from the doors of their houses and before we reached Hirschberg, we had to stop several times while the school children sang songs, shook hands with us and presented me with the gifts which, with much loving care, they had made themselves.

In all, shone the people's friendliness and good nature, in the shining eyes of the children, the steady, smiling faces of old men and women, the cheering youths, the flowers and the flags of my native town.

Hirschberg itself was an undulating sea of colour and movement. The pupils of the Grunau Gliding School and a Luftwaffe detachment were drawn up at the entrance to the town and, in the streets themselves, thousands of people shouted their welcome while the gusty strains of a brass-band surged and faded on the breeze.

So we progressed slowly towards the Town Hall, where, in the Council Chamber, I was presented with the Scroll of Honorary Citizenship, a distinction possessed at that time by one other living person, the world famous poet and play-wright, Gerhart Hauptmann.

In the afternoon, I attended a celebration in my school, seeing again the faces of old friends and many half-forgotten details of the rooms and buildings where I had spent so many happy years. In the sparkling, eager eyes of the girls I seemed to catch a reflection of my own youth.

When my decoration had been announced, I learnt that I had been held up to them as the model pupil of my time—industrious, attentive and well behaved. Unfortunately, this was far from the truth. Though I had enjoyed my schooldays and had learned easily and willingly, I had never been nor wanted to be more than an average pupil and, to my parents' sorrow, my high spirits had earned me each year a rich harvest of black marks in the class-book. A few days before my wartime visit to the school, the girls had discovered this when turning out some old class-books—need I say that their joy was unbounded? However, the dilemma was solved by the Director, who allowed the offending pages to be removed from the class-books, had them bound and then presented them to me himself as a solemn memento of the occasion!

As a conclusion to the festivities, to my great joy the town presented me with a sailplane of the type Grunau-Baby. Later I placed it at the disposal of the Grunau Gliding School, naming it after the unforgettable Otto Bräutigam, who had been killed in action.

I had loved the town of Hirschberg since I was a child, the green slopes of the surrounding hills, its old, gabled houses, the tree-lined walks, the streets and alleyways. Often, when far from home, I had gone back to it in imagination and it was not, therefore, so much the honour done to me that moved me deeply on that day, as the sense of being one with my homeland and its kindly people. This visible demonstration of their love filled me with gratitude, giving me strength and refreshment for many months to come.

## 24. I Crash in a Rocket Plane

TO FLY the rocket plane, Me 163, was to live through a fantasy of Münchhausen. One took off with a roar and a sheet of flame, then shot steeply upwards to find oneself the next moment in the heart of the empyrean.

To sit in the machine when it was anchored to the ground and be surrounded suddenly with that hellish, flame-spewing din, was an experience unreal enough. Through the window of the cabin, I could see the ground crew start back with wide-open mouths and hands over their ears, while, for my part, it was all I could do to hold on as the machine rocked under a ceaseless succession of explosions. I felt as if I were in the grip of some savage power ascended from the

Nether Pit. It seemed incredible than Man could control it.

I sat in the machine on the ground, while the mechanics tested the power-unit, so as to accustom myself to the noise. I had to do this until I was no longer frightened by it and could think and make decisions clearly and coolly without a second's delay, for once I had taken off, the smallest error of judgement might mean the loss of the machine and my own death. In this way, even though, at my first take-off, every nerve in my body, to the very finger-tips, was taut with expectation, my mind was free to co-ordinate the actions necessary to control the plane.

I flew the rocket planes Me 163a and Me 163b in Augsburg, in October, 1942, for the firm of Messerschmitt.

The Me 163a, a tailless plane with rocket power-unit, was the result of some years' experimental work carried out by Dr. Alexander Lippisch and his test-pilot, Flugkapitän Heini Dittmar, at first in Darmstadt and later at Messerschmitt's.

The Me 163a, which was powered by a Walter rocket, was shown to have such excellent qualities on test that it was decided to develop it further, for war-time operational use. Now known as the Me 163b, it was designed to be used as an interceptor to split up enemy bomber formations before attacking the bombers individually.

The Walter rocket built into the plane contained a liquid charge composed of highly concentrated hydrogen peroxide and a special fuel. On coming together in the combustion chamber, the two liquids ignited by spontaneous combustion, producing a temperature of 1,800° Centigrade. They were led into the combustion chamber in a fixed  proportion through tubes under 20 Atmospheres excess pressure. There they were vapourised through twelve jets and produced on combustion a back-thrust of about 4,500 h.p. The thrust was so powerful that at a distance of a hundred yards it was felt on the body as a series of powerful, oscillating blows.

Shortly after leaving the ground, the rocket plane reached a speed of 220 to 250 m.p.h. The undercarriage had then to be jettisoned as there was no room for it to be retracted and its air resistance affected the performance of the plane. To abandon it at an altitude of twenty-five to thirty feet involved the danger that it might bounce back from the ground and strike the fuselage and as the rear portion of the latter contained the rockets and the tanks of high-explosive fluid, any damage to it might have disastrous consequences. After the undercarriage had been dropped, the speed of the aircraft rose in the space of a few seconds to 500 m.p.h. and at this speed, at a climbing angle of 60 to 70 degrees, one could reach a height of 30,000 feet in 1½ minutes.

The Me 163b had excellent flying qualities, better than I had found in any other aircraft. But with its high rate of fuel consumption and a fuel capacity of only 500 gallons—more could not be stored in so small a machine—it could only stay in the air for five or six minutes.

Take-off and landing required the utmost concentration and before they could be undertaken, it was necessary to practice them under tow without the power-unit. As all the fuel was consumed in flight, the plane had always to be landed as a glider and this required some skill and judgement, particularly as the plane had the extremely high landing speed of between 145 and 150 m.p.h.

In Obertraubling, near Regensburg, my friends Opitz and Späthe and myself tested the first Me 163b's to come off the production line. Heini Dittmar, who had taken the prototype through its tests, was unable to come with us as he was lying in hospital with a spine injury obtained on one of his flights. He had been the first to reach and exceed a speed of 625 m.p.h. in this plane.

The test-flights—the first of them without rockets—passed off successfully and I was now to do my fifth. The twin-engined Me 110 towed me across the airfield and a few seconds later we were airborne. At a height of just under thirty feet, I moved the release lever to jettison the undercarriage. Immediately, the whole plane began to shudder violently as if under the influence of a strong turbulence in the air-flow. Red verey lights curved up towards me from the ground: danger! I tried to contact the towing plane by laryngophone but the apparatus was out of order. Then I saw the observer in the gun-turret signalling urgently at me with a white cloth and at the same moment the Me 110 dropped its own undercarriage and retracted it again, then repeated the process—down—up—down—up. So that was what it was, my undercarriage had stuck! Meanwhile, the Me 110 was towing me "round the ring" over the airfield, while I myself had only one desire—to reach a safe height where I could cast off the tow and see if my plane would answer the controls. When I continued to hang on to the tow, the pilot of the Me 110 realised what I wanted and took me up as high as the cloud-base would allow. When we had reached 10,500 feet, I cast off.

By pulling out sharply, I tried to shake off the undercarriage but the plane continued to shudder violently and I could see that the attempt was useless. The only thing I could now do was to try out the plane in its different attitudes of flight to make sure that none of the control surfaces had become affected by the mass of the undercarriage hanging beneath the fuselage and that it was fully controllable.

No pilot entrusted with the testing of a valuable aircraft would ever bale out and abandon it as long as the smallest chance remained of bringing it safely to earth. How and where the miserable contraption had caught itself up on the fuselage, I had no idea, nor could I guess whether it would tear itself through the fuselage when I landed. I could only trust my lucky star and bring the plane to earth, intact, at least, until it touched the ground.

I planned to approach the airfield with height to spare and then, in the last hundred yards or so, side-slip down to the edge of the field. And so I did, until, despite adequate airspeed, the plane suddenly "stalled" and went out of control. In side-slipping, the control surfaces had become useless owing to the turbulent air-currents set up by the irregular mass of the undercarriage.

What happened next left me no time to think. I was still struggling to bring the machine under control when the earth reared up before my eyes. I hunched myself tightly together. We plunged, striking the earth, then, rending and cracking, the machine somersaulted over—lurched—and sagged to a stop.

The first thing I realised was that I was not hanging in my harness and therefore the machine was right-side up. Quite automatically, my right hand opened the cabin roof—it was intact. Cautiously, I ran my hand down my left arm and hand, then slowly along my sides, chest and legs. To my thankful amazement, nothing was missing and all seemed in working order. I felt as if I had returned to the familiar world from some far-distant shore . . .

Then I noticed a stream of blood coursing down from the direction of my head. Feeling no pain, I started to track the stream to its source and as my fingers moved upwards, across my face, they came upon it—at the place where my nose had been was now nothing but an open cleft. Each time I breathed, bubbles of air and blood formed along its edge.

I tried turning my head sideways and immediately, black shutters snapped over my eyes. Without moving my head again, I fetched pencil and pad from a pocket and drew a sketch, showing the course of events leading to the crash. Then I took out a handkerchief and tied it round my face at nose level, so that when they arrived, the rescue party would be spared the shock of seeing my condition. Then darkness closed over me.

When I regained consciousness, I saw the figures of my friends standing before me in a white blur. I pulled myself together in an effort to reassure them. And still I could feel no pain.

From the airfield they took me by car to Regensburg, to the Hospital of the Sisters of Mercy. The X-ray plates revealed serious damage: the skull was fractured in four places in the basal area and in two places in the facial area, involving compression of the brain, displacement of the upper jaw-bones and separation of the bones of the nose.

I had the great good fortune to be in the hands of a first-class surgeon, Dr. Bodewig, and the last thing I remembered was seeing the walls of the operating theatre.

When I awoke, I was lying in a bright, friendly room. I saw faces, smiling indeed, but looking strangely concerned. My head was thickly bandaged. Only the swollen lips and the blue, bruised rims of the eyes could be seen.

Very slowly my mind cleared. "Mother," I thought and although my aunt, Käthe von Cochenhausen, was standing there beside the doctor and that was like a piece of home, I felt a sudden lurch of home-sickness.

Next morning, when I opened my eyes, my mother was kneeling beside my bed. Now I knew I was safe.

I could see from the doctor's expression that things were not well with me. The thought caused me no distress but if the end was at hand, I wanted to know so as to be prepared for it. To my question, the doctor gave only an evasive answer, so I asked to see my very close friend, Edelgard von Berg, who was herself a capable surgeon and worked under Professor Gorband in the Robert Koch Hospital in Berlin. She, I knew, would tell me the truth.

My mother telephoned her and she promised to come at once. She left Berlin by car and, on reaching Leipzig, telephoned to let us know she was on the way. Then we waited, hour after hour, waited, till my happy anticipation of seeing her again gradually curdled into sick foreboding, waited, until at last my mother had to tell me the news—and on hearing it, I fainted. My friend had had a car crash and was dead.

For a long time my condition was very serious. I knew it without being told. Nevertheless, I felt no fear for now I was immersed in a new life, all that formerly had seemed important lying remote and insignificant beyond its bounds, while I lay pillowed in stillness. My mother knew of this and stayed with me, sharing my new and passionless world. She could never know how much she helped me at this time, for soon I was to be harrowed ceaselessly, not by pain but by anxious, fear-ridden thoughts that chased incessantly through my badly injured brain. To be lying helpless while on all sides ominous events were unfolding filled me with despair. I tried not to think, for thought was physically painful and emotion of any kind endangered my recovery. Here again, it was my mother and she alone who was able to calm me, she alone who finally persuaded me to abandon thought and lay my mind at rest, placing it in God's Hand. Gradually, in my darkness, she relighted the candles of hope and, through her undaunted faith that one day I would fly again, she brought me to the path that was to lead me back to life.

For over five months I lay in hospital in Regensburg, receiving every day so many tokens of friendship and love that I was almost put to shame. Dr. Bodewig took endless pains in treating me and the Sisters of Mercy nursed me with untiring devotion.

A few days after my accident, I received the Iron Cross, First Class.

By March, 1943, I was well enough to be discharged from hospital, although my recovery was by no means yet complete and it seemed doubtful whether it ever would be.

I was offered a choice of sanatoria in which to convalesce, but I declined them all. If I was to get better it would have to be in my own way. I arranged, instead, to go to Saalberg to the house of some friends that lay hidden in a great park-like garden almost half way up the mountain slopes of the Riesengebirge. The house was now empty—my friends only used it in summer—and I should be able, as I wanted, to be quite alone. After spending a few happy days, still as a stretcher-case, with my parents in Hirschberg, I transferred to this hermitage at the beginning of April, taking with me as protection a club and a pistol. Only I knew how ill I still was. None could guess that my head still ached incessantly or that the shortest car or train journey made me feel sick and giddy. Once in the complete freedom and utter quiet of my new abode, however, I hoped gradually to recover my health.

After a few days spent in a timeless peacefulness, I started to try and overcome my attacks of giddiness and recover my sense of balance. The house had a gabled roof of unusually steep pitch and a narrow flight of steps which led from the ground to a chimney stack, protruding above it. Very slowly and cautiously, I climbed the steps to the top and seated myself astride the ridge, my hands firmly clinging to the chimney stack and my eyes closed so as not to lose my balance. Then, opening my eyes, I focused them successively on each row of tiles down to the verge of the roof and from there, transferred them to the ground. Then I repeated the exercise down the other side of the roof. First to the right—then to the left.

At first, my climbs to the roof cost me inordinate exertion and left me totally exhausted. But I went on repeating them day after day until gradually I began to find it easier. In a while, I found I no longer needed to hold on to the chimney stack and I could let my eyes wander freely over the roof and the neighbouring countryside. Venturing farther and farther away from the chimney, at last, after four weeks, I was able to push myself along the whole length of the ridge without a trace of giddiness.

Some days, by way of variety, I would transfer my exercises to a pine-tree, trying to climb up it from branch to branch. Here, too, at first, I soon reached the limits of my strength and then, remembering my childhood days, when no tree had been too high for me to climb, sometimes in my weakness I would almost surrender to despair.

To build up my strength, I undertook as well daily walks along paths leading to the mountain slopes. Often I had to turn back before going far through exhaustion and agonising headaches but here, too, my strength gradually increased until finally I succeeded in reaching the line of the mountain ridge.

Still finding it difficult to concentrate and co-ordinate my thoughts, I sent for my secretary and dictated something to her every day, as a form of mind-training.

When, at last, I felt I had recovered sufficiently, I asked the commander of the School of Aerial Warfare at Breslau-Schöngarten if I might fly some of his machines to get myself back into training. He agreed on the understanding that I would not overtax my strength and also that the matter should be kept secret from my doctors. I started by flying a glider in towed flight, a task which I found myself able to do without the slightest difficulty. Then I flew powered aircraft, diving each time from a greater height to see if my head could tolerate rapid changes in air pressure. For the same purpose, I attempted steep turns, spins and aerobatics. Within a few weeks, my flying capabilities were back to normal. It seemed a miracle and when I told the doctors in Hirschberg, they looked on me almost as a medical curiosity. But to me, all that mattered was—I was fit to fly again.

## 25. Conversations with Himmler

AMONG THE flowers and other gifts which I received in hospital in Regensburg, there arrived one day a small parcel from Himmler, containing a slab of chocolate and a bottle of fruit juice. It was accompanied by a personal letter expressing good wishes for a rapid recovery and urging me to omit nothing that might help to restore me to full health.

Feeling dubious and somewhat embarrassed, my mother and I considered these objects, so simple and unostentatious beside the large and formal looking flower arrangements that others had sent. In our family, we had always avoided mentioning the name of Himmler: my mother saw in him the adversary of Christianity and he could therefore have nothing in common with us.

As long as I was in hospital, these small gifts were repeated at regular intervals, accompanied always by a few lines in Himmler's own hand, so simply and unaffectedly worded that even my mother was not unimpressed. Finally, she became convinced that the picture which we had formed of Himmler might be a false one, based, as it was, on what we had been told of his official activities. Anxious, as always, not to be unjust in her judgements, she therefore urged me, as soon as I had recovered, to call on Himmler personally to thank him for his kindness. I was able to do so in July, 1943, arriving by air at his headquarters in East Prussia in the evening, shortly before dinner time.

Himmler came out to meet me, greeting me in a friendly way with an invitation to dine with himself and his officers. During the meal, I noticed and was surprised by the frank and easy relations that seemed to exist among the officers and between them and their superior.

Afterwards, Himmler invited me to his study. For the first time I was now alone with him. So that my sincere expression of thanks for his kindness should not be the cause of misunderstanding, I admitted that in my family the mention of his name had always aroused trepidation.

Himmler listened calmly and then asked:

"Do you always form your judgements so hastily, Frau Hanna?"

He brought an arm-chair for me and seated himself directly opposite.

"What exactly do you find in my name to alarm you?"

"I hardly know where to start," I replied. "For one thing, how can you bring yourself to try and root out of men's hearts their most sacred beliefs when you have nothing remotely comparable in worth to replace them?"

For reply, Himmler delivered a sharp attack on the plausibility of the Christian doctrine, showing an intimate knowledge of the Bible and supporting his arguments with many unfamiliar examples, of which I lacked sufficient knowledge to be able to refute him.

I therefore returned to the crux of the matter.

"We are concerned with a religious belief," I said emphatically. "I cannot compel you to share this belief, but in your position you should respect and not interfere with the religious feelings of others."

I continued on this theme, although I realised that I would not be able to persuade Himmler to change his attitude. But I wanted to tell him frankly my opinion on these questions.

We then turned to another problem, about which my

feelings were strong, his attitude to women and marriage. I reproached him for looking at the matter from a purely racial and biological stand-point, considering woman only as a bearer of children and through his directives to the SS, about which, admittedly, I had only heard rumours, tending to undermine morality and destroy the sanctity of marriage. Such an attitude would be bound, in my opinion, to bring about the downfall of a people.

Himmler replied to my charges factually and at considerable length. He assured me that he shared my views entirely. His policy had been misrepresented and misinterpreted, either unintentionally or from deliberate malice. It was very important, he said, that these tendentious rumours should not get about, particularly at the present time, when he was considering the introduction into the SS of the "Stabshelferinnen" organisation* already employed in the Army. He himself had drawn up the rules governing their employment, adhering closely to the pattern of the Finnish Lottas, whose employment and bearing in war were well known to be exemplary. I did not fail to point out to Himmler that, in spite of what he had said, appearances were in general against him.

During our conversation, which lasted for several hours, I had an opportunity to look at my surroundings. Himmler's study was furnished simply but with the utmost good taste. I was particularly struck by some fine old engravings on the walls. Noticing my interest, Himmler gave me a detailed account of each picture: they represented figures and scenes from Prussian history.

He then went on to tell me about Allach, the new firm of porcelain manufacturers, showing me some of their designs which he had evolved himself. Among these, he produced a Christmas platter and asked me what I thought of it. I said I did not like it. He did not seem offended, but pursed his lips in thought for a moment and then announced his decision—he would cancel the order for its manufacture.

* A woman's organisation, similar in function to the A.T.S., but confined to clerical work in the army administrative staff.

Before I left, Himmler thanked me for my outspokenness, which he assured me was something new to him, obtaining from me the promise that, if I had any more criticisms or objections to raise at any time, I would not hesitate to bring them to his notice. This promise I kept.

In October, 1944, my old flying comrade, Peter Riedel, who was now in the German Embassy in Stockholm, called on me at the Flying Club in Berlin. In a state of considerable agitation, he threw a booklet down on the table:

"If you want to know what's going on in Germany, look at this! This is what we find on our desks in the Embassy!"

I glanced through the booklet, which concerned the gas-chambers. I was beside myself:

"And you believe this?" I asked, furious. "In the First World War, enemy propaganda smeared the German soldier with every imaginable barbarity—now it has come to gas-chambers!"

My emotion strongly impressed my friend.

"I'll believe that from you," he said, but asked me to inform Himmler about it immediately.

I telephoned Himmler, obtaining permission to visit him at his headquarters in the field. Arrived there, I placed the booklet before him.

"What do you say to this, Reichsführer?"

Himmler picked it up and flicked over the pages. Then, without change of expression, he looked up, eyeing me quietly:

"And you believe this, Frau Hanna?"

"No, of course not. But you must do something to counter it. You can't let them shoulder this onto Germany. '

Himmler laid the booklet on the table, then looked at me once more:

"You are right," he said.

## 26.  With the Troops on the Russian Front

WHEN THE disaster of Stalingrad was announced in
February, 1943, the whole German people realised
that they were engaged in a life and death struggle. After
Stalingrad, the shadows began visibly to descend over
Germany and in spite of official propaganda, which was still
turned to victory, month by month the feeling grew that the
end was inexorably approaching.

In the long months in hospital, I had followed these
developments with increasing concern and when I was
restored to health, I at once reported back to Göring. To my
surprise, I received an invitation to his house in the Ober-
salzberg, where he and his wife entertained me to lunch. We
talked about my crash and about the Me 163. To my horror,
I discovered that, on the subject of the rocket plane, Göring
had been completely misinformed, believing it to be already
in mass production, although in reality it was not yet out of
the experimental stage. I tried to tell him the true state of
affairs, but he would not listen. Instead, he became furiously
angry and stalked out of the room. Feeling instinctively that
even an unpalatable truth is better than self-deception, his
wife finally succeeded in calming him but the conversation
thereafter remained formal and stilted and it became only
too clear that Göring did not wish his comforting illusions to
be disturbed. I never visited him again.

Profoundly depressed by this incident, I returned to my
task of test-pilot. The rocket plane was now being tested at
Bad Zwischenahn in Oldenburg and it was there that the call
reached me from Colonel General Ritter von Greim, asking
me to come to him on the Eastern Front, where he and his
men were engaged in a struggle of almost superhuman
proportions.

Greim was commanding an Air Fleet in the middle sector.

185

As an airman in the First World War, he had received the highest decoration for valour, the "Pour Le Mérite," allied to great courage, he had a high veneration for life and would never expose any of his men to danger unless it was absolutely necessary, demanding of them simply what circumstances required. Both officers and men, therefore, looked upon him as a father.

He had now the exacting task of supplying air support for his sector of the front with insufficient aircraft and it was all the more important, therefore, to maintain a high morale among his men. He knew that this could only be achieved by personal example and he himself had been constantly among the men in the foremost positions. Nevertheless, he felt convinced that a visit from a woman on whom military decorations had been conferred would achieve even more.

I reached his headquarters in November, 1943. They were in a wood in the neighbourhood of Orscha. Throughout the night, even in my sleep, I could hear the ceaseless roll and thunder of the guns from the nearby front. Next morning, at dawn, von Greim and I set off to visit his advanced Ack-Ack positions, which were then awaiting a large-scale enemy attack. We flew in a Fieseler-Storch reconnaissance machine, escorted by a second. It was icily cold.

For the first time, I was now having direct experience of war, as a soldier sees it. To avoid being detected by the enemy, we hedge-hopped all the way until, a short distance from the front line, we exchanged the "Storch" for an armoured car which brought us close up to the front-line positions. The last stretch we had to do on foot, working our way forward in short, crouching runs, as the area was under direct observation by the enemy.

Hardly had we reached the Ack-Ack positions, than the Russians opened up a heavy bombardment. Automatically, everyone vanished into the ground, while all around us the air whistled and shuddered and crashed. When our own guns started to roar their answer and, shortly after, a formation of Russian planes began to bomb our positions, I felt, in my terror, as though I wanted to creep right in on myself. When, finally, to this inferno were added the most horrible sounds of all, the yells of the wounded, I felt certain that not one of us would emerge alive. Cowering in a hole in the ground, it was in vain that I tried to stop the persistent knocking of my knees.

When at last the bombardment ceased and we could leave our burrows, I helped to dress the wounded. Then we went on, visiting, during the pause in the firing, each individual gun-site. The danger had been considered too great for me to go, but having seen the men's eyes light up at sight of me, I knew now what it meant to them to receive this unexpected visitor from home, and I refused to be left behind.

On that first day, which I shall never forget, I had realised what a handicap it was that I had no front-line experience. Surrounded by danger, the soldier at least knew how best to meet it, whereas I did not. The result was that I felt continually on edge.

On the following day, therefore, while the enemy artillery was firing, I asked an N.C.O. to teach me to distinguish between the sounds of the enemy shells and our own. Taking cover behind a tank, I pressed back my fear and listened strenuously, as the voice of the N.C.O. came clear and calm through the thunder and wail of the shells:

"Ours"—"Theirs"—"Shell-burst, no danger."—"Stand still!"—"Look out!"—"Down——!" And on top of his words, the shell exploded and the earth heaved into the air.

On days when the weather was too bad for operational flights, I visited isolated Luftwaffe units in the area Orscha-Witebsk, flying in a Fieseler Storch. The men accepted me as one of themselves, poured out to me their questions, worries and thoughts. When they asked about the war situation, I tried hard not to raise false hopes.

I spent three weeks in all visiting Luftwaffe units in the midst of their battle on the Eastern Front. Flying beneath grey skies over measureless expanses of open country occupied by partisans, talking with weary and anxious men in huts and holes in the ground, the hand-clasps of those from my own homeland, the agony, the endurance—and the cold: all this will not fade from my mind.

## 27. I Fly the V1

MUCH INK has flowed on the subject of the piloted V1. For years the world press had indulged in sensational reports on the hazardous methods of testing this man-flown robot and the hair-raising uses to which it was to be put. But the real reasons which led to placing a pilot in the pilotless plane and the purpose for which it was intended have never been accurately given to the public.

The story begins in August, 1943, in Berlin. One day, over lunch at the Flying Club, I came across two old friends. One of them was an aeronautical medical specialist, and the other, a very skilful and experienced glider-pilot.

Our conversation centred on the progress of the war, which was causing us deep uneasiness. We were agreed that time was not on Germany's side, for every day that passed brought a further drain on her diminishing resources. One after another, towns and cities were crumpling under the Allied air attacks, the transport system and the production centres were being systematically destroyed, raw materials were becoming increasingly difficult to procure, while the death roll continually mounted.

Moreover the Morgenthau Plan was not unknown in Germany and fully realising that a lost war would involve the innocent as well as the guilty in the same tragic fate, our desire was the same—to do all in our power to avert it.

But how much did lie in our power? For months this question had been occupying my thoughts and, as I discovered at lunch that day, the thoughts of my friends.

We were agreed on our answer. It was clear to us that underlying and determining the course of this war was the razor-keen battle of the scientists and technicians and that a change in Germany's favour could only be brought about by success in this field.

We also believed that the war must be brought to an early end if Germany were to be saved from disaster and that this could only be secured through a negotiated peace. To prepare the ground for negotiation, it would be necessary to weaken considerably the enemy's military strength.

This could only be done from the air and only, we believed, if volunteers were forthcoming to pilot a suitable projectile into the centre of its target, destroying it totally and making repair or re-equipment impossible. By this means it should be possible to deliver, while sparing the enemy civil population, a rapid succession of devasting blows at generating stations, waterworks, key production centres, and, in the event of invasion, at naval and merchant shipping.

Though such men, if they could be found, would be volunteering for certain death, it would be no task for mere dare-devils, indifferent to the full significance of their action, nor for blind fanatics, nor for the disenchanted and the life-weary who might see here their chance to make a theatrical exit. This Operation Suicide would require men who were ready to sacrifice themselves in the conviction that only by this means could their country be saved. Finally, an effervescent idealism was also not enough, for self-sacrifice was not the end but a part only of the means, the other being calm and accurate calculation.

All three of us were agreed that the realisation of the project depended on whether a plane could be developed which would be completely and absolutely dependable, and could be proved to be so. Without this, the whole idea would become repugnant, as entailing a frivolous and senseless destruction of life.

I must mention at this point that nothing had so far been heard in Germany of the Japanese Suicide-Pilots. Nevertheless, the conversation with my friends that August day seemed to show that the conception of suicide-pilots was more widespread in Germany than any of us had imagined. When it came to calling for volunteers, that impression was strikingly confirmed. We found them everywhere. Most of them were married and fathers of families and were robust,

uncomplicated individuals. As they saw it, the sacrifice of
their lives would be as nothing compared with the millions,
both soldiers and civilians, who would die if the war was
allowed to continue. Moreover, they were convinced that the
sacrifice was necessary if their wives and children, and their
country, were to be saved.

We concealed our thoughts from strangers and those outside our own immediate circle. Nevertheless, it continually
widened as more and more of our associates were initiated
into our plans. That we were often misunderstood was only
to be expected, for our plan held no appeal for seekers after
fame and offered no chance of a successful outcome to those
who felt inclined for a gamble with death. Here was required
nothing less than the complete conquest of self.

If the plan were prepared on a large enough scale and
with sufficient care, it must be possible, we thought, to bring
about the complete destruction of the enemy's vital war
centres and therefore we hoped that those in authority would
examine without delay the practicability of our ideas so that,
before submitting them to Hitler, we could work out complete and accurate technical details. But we had little conception of the obstacles and difficulties we were to encounter.

I first approached Field-Marshal Milch, Deputy-Chief of
the Luftwaffe and Göring's Second-in-Command. He refused
point-blank to consider the idea. In his opinion, it was contrary to the German mentality to undertake a task in which
the chance of personal survival was nil. I found it impossible
in a formal interview to persuade him that self-sacrifice with
the object of saving others' lives was fully justified and contented myself with the request that he leave the question to
the conscience of the individual volunteers, whom, after all,
it primarily concerned.

Next, we approached the Aeronautical Research Institute,
the Director of which undertook to call a conference of all
interested scientists, technicians and tacticians in order to
examine our plan.

The conference took place in the winter of 1943/1944

under the chairmanship of the Director. Specialists from all branches of war industry were present, experts on explosives, on torpedoes, navigational and radio technicians, maritime engineers, naval officers and aircraft designers. The Officers commanding Fighter Squadrons and Bomber Squadrons each sent a representative. Even medical specialists attended.

The plan was declared to be fundamentally sound, both in its technical and operational aspects. At this conference, the employment of an adapted Vi was considered, but rejected in favour of a converted glider-bomb and, in order to save time, it was decided to use a type already in production, the Messerschmitt 328. Depending on the type of target to be attacked and the methods adopted for approaching it, the explosive charge was to be built into the tail of the plane and was to be either a specially constructed bomb or an adapted torpedo-bomb.

Permission to start work on construction had now to be obtained from the highest authority of all—in other words, we had to interest Hitler in our plan. As we had foreseen, none among my circle of friends succeeded in obtaining an interview with him but, on 28th February, 1944, an un-looked-for opportunity presented itself. I received a summons to attend at the Berghof, Hitler's mountain chalet, to be presented with a certificate to mark my award of the Iron Cross (First Class).

When the day arrived, Hitler invited me to take tea with him. It was served in the big room overlooking the country-side of Berchtesgaden where he usually held his tea-parties and the only other person present was his Luftwaffe Adju-tant, Colonel von Below.

I did not hesitate to take this opportunity of putting for-ward our plan, but the conversation which developed as a consequence took a somewhat unexpected course. Hitler's first reaction was to reject completely the idea of suicide missions. He did not consider the war situation sufficiently serious to warrant them and, in any case, believed that this was not the right psychological moment for the idea to be acceptable to public opinion. The decision as to when, and if, that moment did arrive, he reserved for himself.

Hitler expounded his views on the subject in a series of lengthy monologues, supporting his argument with numerous illustrations from the pages of history. These were certainly recounted in compelling and memorable phraseology, but on reflection I could see that, while superficially apposite, they were, in reality, irrelevant. I therefore ventured the remark that I felt the situation in which Germany now found herself was without historical precedent and could only be remedied by new and extraordinary methods.

My objection caused Hitler to continue his lecture on a somewhat different theme, and to expatiate on the use of jet-aircraft. Now I knew for a fact that, in Germany, jet propulsion was still only in the early stages of development and that many months would pass before jet-aircraft reached the production stage, and many months more before they became operational.

Hitler, I could see, was living in some remote and nebulous world of his own and the appalling implications of this discovery suddenly burst upon me. Forgetting for a moment the respect due to his position, I broke in on his reflections in mid-sentence and objected loudly: "Mein Führer, you are speaking of the grandchild of an embryo." Hitler looked up with a start and stared at me questioningly.

I did not wait for him to break the painful silence which now ensued—I caught sight of his Adjutant's face, glazed with horror—but went straight on to tell Hitler the facts, of which I was quite certain, that proved him to be under a misconception.

But I had quite destroyed Hitler's good humour. Although he retained a conventional politeness, his face wore a disgruntled expression and his voice sounded peevish as he gave me to understand that I was not sufficiently informed of the situation to be able to form a correct appreciation.

The discussion on which I had pinned all my hopes now threatened to end in disaster, but too much was at stake for me to give up without trying once more to obtain Hitler's

agreement to our project. I returned to the subject of
suicide-pilots and, reminding him of his statement at the
start of the conversation, asked permission for us to start
experimental work on the type of plane to be used so that
when Hitler decided that the right moment had arrived to
employ it, the suicide attacks could be started at once.
Hitler then agreed to do so, with the proviso that we were
not to worry him further during the development stage.

Ten minutes later, I was on my way back to Berchtesgaden
where my friends were anxiously awaiting me.

From now on, responsibility for the development of the
project lay with the Chief of the General Staff of the Luftwaffe, General Korten. He attached the personnel of the
Suicide Group to one of the existing Luftwaffe squadrons,
giving instructions that they were to be taken on the estab-
lishment as a special unit. Of the thousands who had volunteered as suicide-pilots, to start with, only about seventy
were called up. The remainder were to be embodied when
the technical details had been completed, the operational
tasks and tactical methods worked out and an officer
appointed to command the Group.

Volunteers were required to sign the following declaration:

"I HEREBY VOLUNTARILY APPLY TO BE ENROLLED IN THE
SUICIDE GROUP AS PILOT OF A HUMAN GLIDER-BOMB. I FULLY
UNDERSTAND THAT EMPLOYMENT IN THIS CAPACITY WILL
ENTAIL MY OWN DEATH."

I, of course, signed this declaration at once, but was
persuaded by my friends to delay for a time my enrolment in
the Group itself so as to avoid having to obey military orders.
That this decision was a wise one became apparent later
when, the command and methods of the Group developing
in a sense contrary to our ideas, I was able to appeal to
higher authority for a change of policy over the heads of
those who were directly responsible.

All technical preparations concerning the Suicide Group
were placed in the hands of the Reich Air Ministry. By great
good fortune, the Head of the particular Section entrusted
with this work, Heinz Kensche, had himself volunteered as a

suicide-pilot and I was invited to become jointly responsible
with him for the testing of the prototype planes and equipment.

We carried out the first tests at Hörsching, near Linz, on
the type which my friends and I had first earmarked for
suicide attacks, the Messerschmitt 328. Originally designed
as a long-range fighter or light bomber, the Me 328 had been
produced by the firm of Messerschmitt in co-operation with
an Aeronautical Research Station. We carried out tests
using two Argus-Schmitt jet-engines as the power-unit, but
after one or two flights, further experiments with the
powered Me 328 were abandoned by the Ministry.

We now tested whether the Me 328 could be used, without
its power-unit, as a human glider-bomb. It was a single-
seater plane with a very short wing-span of about fifteen feet.
The lift-drag ratio was approximately 1:12 at 150 m.p.h.
and 1:5 at 470 m.p.h. The Me 328 could not take off alone
and in the tests was carried pick-a-back on a Dornier 217
bomber to a height between 9,000 and 18,000 feet. It was
possible for the pilot of the Me 328 to detach himself, without
leaving his seat, from the back of the Do 217 in mid-air and
the take-off then presented no difficulties. The characteristics
of the Me 328 fulfilled the requirements of a glider-bomb,
namely, good visibility, comfort, first-class manoeuvrability,
structural and navigational stability.

We finished the tests in April, 1944. An aircraft factory in
Thuringia was now to receive the contract for mass production of the plane. But, for reasons still unknown to me,
production was never properly started and not a single plane
reached us from the factory.

We now bitterly regretted not having carried out experimental tests of the piloted V1 jointly with the Me 328. And
at this stage of the war, where could we hope to find effective
support for the continuation of our plans?

Unexpectedly the help came. One day in April, 1944, Otto
Skorzeny introduced himself to me over the telephone and
said he was anxious to meet me. This was the man whose
name had become a by-word as the pilot who had rescued

Mussolini by helicopter from an hotel in the Abruzzi Mountains where he was held prisoner by the Badoglio Government. Skorzeny, it appeared, had recently been told by
Himmler about our project and had himself been concerned
in the development of special weapons. He was already in
contact with those in the Navy who saw in the use of one-
man torpedoes and frogmen a chance of bringing about a
last-minute change in the course of the war in Germany's
favour. Quite independently of us, Skorzeny had also come
on the idea of the piloted V1 and had been anxious to meet
me in order to discuss it.

When he saw how the situation lay, Skorzeny set to work
in characteristic fashion, sweeping aside all objections and
obstacles with the same simple pretext, "Hitler had vested
him with full powers and had expressly called for a daily
progress-report."

Even to-day it seems to me almost incredible that a team
of engineers and constructors succeeded in converting a V1
in four or five days. The piloted V1 was given the code-name
of "Reichenberg" and was kept strictly on the secret list.
Only a few people knew of its existence and not even those
who worked on the normal V1 were let into the secret.

Various adaptations of the pilotless V1 were constructed,
using the standard components already in production. The
first of the new models was a single-seater V1 with cushioned
skids and pilot's seat placed directly behind the wing. As
this model was for training, it was also provided with a
power-unit and landing-flaps.

The second model was a two-seater V1 with one seat
placed in front of and the other behind the wing. It was fitted
with dual controls and, being intended for training-school
use, had no power-unit.

Landing a V1 was at all times an extremely difficult and
dangerous operation and, even when specially trained, pilots
of average ability could never be certain of surviving the
attempt. If our project was to come to fruition at all, we had
to do our best to keep down the fatality rate among the men
on whom the entire training scheme depended, namely, the

instructors, and these were accordingly most carefully picked from among the best of the volunteers.

The third model was the single-seater, operational V1, with power-unit, but without skids or landing-flaps. In other words, it could not be landed,—its first flight would also, inevitably, be the last.

I volunteered to test the prototype, but the experimental station at Rechlin insisted on using their own pilots.

On a warm summer's day, Otto Skorzeny and I attended the first test at Lärz. On arriving, we found the plane ready to start. The V1 was hanging under the right wing of the Heinkel III bomber. Since the Allies had captured the launching sites in the Pas de Calais area, the pilotless V1's had no longer been launched by catapult as their radius of action was insufficient to carry them to their objective from platforms inside Germany. They were now carried by an He III and launched from the mother-plane from a point nearer their target. A catapult start was also out of the question for the piloted V1 on account of its high acceleration (about $17g^{+}$), and it was therefore to be launched in the same way.

Fascinated, we followed the Heinkel as it took off with its burden and climbed higher and higher. Then the moment came when we saw the test-pilot detach his plane from the bomber and drop away in the V1 like some small, swift bird.

The pilot flew in tight turns until, on a dead-straight course, he began to lose height, gliding at an ever steeper angle towards the earth. It did not take us long to realize that this behaviour of the machine was in no way intended by the pilot. The machine disappeared from sight and shortly after we heard an explosion in the distance and saw a column of black smoke rising in the summer air. For half an hour we waited, fearing to hear the news, until at last the report came through that the pilot was severely injured but still alive.

It transpired that the crash had been caused, not by some structural defect in the aircraft, but through the pilot's own

+ Symbol expressing value of acceleration due to gravity.

inadvertance. He had unintentionally pressed the catch to
the sliding hood of the cockpit and, half stunned by the force
of the air-current, had lost control over the plane.

The day after, a second pilot took off in the VI. He, too,
came to grief, though escaping with his life.

From then on, Heinz Kensche and I were allowed to take
over the prototype tests of the piloted VI.

My first flight passed without incident and the next eight
or ten flights were also successful, though not without their
awkward moments.

On one occasion, for example, the pilot of the He III had
just released me from beneath the bomber's wing, when his
plane grazed the rear of the VI. There was a loud rending
noise, as if the tail of my plane had been broken right off.
Though only just able to continue to control the plane, I
managed to make a smooth landing, finding, when I inspected it, that the tail had been crumpled and twisted to the
right through an angle of almost thirty degrees. It seemed a
miracle that it had not come right off.

On another occasion, I was testing the behaviour of the
two-seater model of the VI at a wide range of speed along an
inclined flight-path, flying at speeds up to 530 m.p.h. During
the test, a sack of sand, which had been wedged in the front
seat on my instructions to supply extra weight, somehow
broke loose and shifted position. In blissful ignorance, I tried
to flatten out at speed and suddenly found that I could not
move the elevator. I had not enough height, or time, to be
able to bale out by parachute and had to risk all on a last,
faint chance of saving myself and the plane. Just before the
machine reached the ground, I pushed her nose down and
then, with all the response I could get from the elevator,
quickly pulled out again. This manoeuvre checked the plane
just enough for me to be able to make a landing, though an
extremely hard one which splintered the skids and the hull. I
emerged without a scratch . . .

On yet another test-flight, I was trying out the VI fully
loaded at high speeds. For this test we had built a water-tank
into the hull. As the landing skids were too fragile to stand up

to the shock of landing when heavily loaded (for the operational machine would be crashed straight into its target) we had fitted a draining plug in the tank, operated by moving a lever, so that the water could be let out before landing. Otherwise, the pilot would most certainly receive an unpleasant surprise.

I started to test the V1 at about 18,000 feet—with the consequence that the draining hole froze up. When I tried to move the lever to open the drain-plug at 4,500 feet, I found that it would not budge. The plane was now gliding rapidly downwards and as no engine was fitted to this model, time was all-important. In a frenzy of desperation, I gripped and clawed at the lever till my fingers were bleeding. The earth was stretching up nearer and nearer towards me. At last, with only a few hundred feet to go, the lever suddenly moved and there was just time to drain out most of the water. Lucky!

When the tests had been satisfactorily completed, we began to train the men we had chosen to be instructors of the other volunteers, using the two-seater model of the V1. Though any average pilot could fly the V1 without difficulty once it was in the air, to land it called for exceptional skill, in that it had a very high landing speed and, moreover, in training it was the glider model, without engine, that was usually employed. The training period, therefore, made heavy demands on all concerned.

But meanwhile, the stream of time rolled on and rolling, bore all our efforts to oblivion, confronting Germany with new and menacing developments. The Invasion had begun.

Now that the Invasion had been launched, neither the Me 328 nor the piloted V1 could be used as we had intended. We realized that the decisive moment had been missed. And now that it was too late, we realized, too, that, from the very start the obstacles that were put in our way were greater than our will to carry the plan through. Among these were the misunderstandings and the clash of personalities among the very people who were working hardest for its success.

A yet more formidable difficulty was the total failure on

the part of higher authority to appreciate that the Suicide Group was no stunt, but a collection of brave, clear-headed and intelligent Germans who seriously believed, after careful thought and calculation, that by sacrificing their own lives they might save many times that number of their fellow-countrymen and ensure some kind of future for their children.

But this conception was too cold to kindle the imaginations of Himmler and Goebbels. Himmler suggested that the suicide-pilots should be recruited among the incurably diseased, the neurotics and the criminals so that through a voluntary death they might redeem their "honour." Goebbels hasted to exploit the Group for propaganda purposes by summoning its members to his Ministry and reciting to them a premature panegyric on the theme of heroism. Is it surprising that when the suicide-pilots were finally ready to go into action, it was already too late?

## 28. The Last Journey to Berlin

IN OCTOBER, 1944, I was injured on my way to the shelter in an air-raid on Berlin and was taken to a Luftwaffe hospital, where it was found I had concussion and a torn capsule of the left elbow-joint. Once again, I was prevented from flying for several weeks.

I had only been a few days in hospital when I heard that Heinz Kensche, who had "stood-in" for me as test-pilot of the V1, had had to bale out on one of his flights. I could not rest until I had found out more about his experiences and the reason why the V1 had crashed. And so, while doctors and nurses believed me to be taking a convalescent stroll through the Tiergarten, I seized my opportunity and, driving to Adlershof, where my plane was kept, made a quick hop to my friends at Lärz.

On hearing of this trip, the doctor forbade me to leave the hospital. Cut off from the outside world, I was continually pressed by the picture of bomb-shattered Berlin as I had seen it from the air and by the ever more certain foreboding that the city was not yet out of its ordeal and that worse was to come.

It might finally become impossible, I thought, to land an aircraft in Berlin at all, for how would a pilot be able to find his bearings if yet more areas of the city were destroyed and what remained lay shrouded in fire and smoke? Yet that might be the very time when air transport was most needed, to take out wounded, for example, or for urgent and special missions.

I discussed this question with Colonel Rudel, who was in the same hospital as I recovering from a leg amputation. My idea was to use a helicopter because it can take off and land in the smallest space, on a flat roof, for instance. Even the platform of a nearby Ack-Ack tower might be enough.

Rudel and I inspected the tower. We thought it should be possible to make a landing on it, even in the smoke and turmoil of battle, when visibility would be almost nil. But we had to remember that there would be no radio beam to guide us in.

As soon as I was out of hospital, I went into training and systematically flew in to the Ack-Ack tower from a variety of landmarks on the outskirts of the city, in all weathers and at very low altitudes. From each point I took the compass-bearing of the tower and carefully memorised it. Soon, every hole, every corner, every bomb-shattered roof on each of the approaches to the tower was familiar to me and I knew that in no matter what conditions, by day or night, in fog or fire, I should find my way to it with absolute certainty.

These activities reached, in due course, the ears of General-Oberst Ritter von Greim, Colonel-General in the Luftwaffe.

In January, 1945, the war was entering its final stages. For months the German armies had struggled vainly to stem the all-engulfing avalanche. In the West, as in the East, Allied troops had for some time now been on German soil.

On the Russian front, the war was fought out to a bitter end. At Breslau an attempt was made to throw a breakwater before the surging tide of the Russian armies, the whole city being declared a beleaguered fortress and placed under siege law. It was, however, clear to all that the attempt to hold Breslau could never succeed and there was great concern and anxiety over the fate of the population.

My home was in Silesia and so when I received a radio message from Breslau asking me to fly into the city, I did not hesitate. At that time, in the middle of February, there was still one airfield open, though constantly under enemy air attack. I stayed a day and a night in Breslau and then flew back with urgent despatches to Berlin. I flew for the second time to Breslau, now completely encircled, a fortnight later, being accompanied on this trip by State-Secretary Naumann. On our way, we touched down at Schweidnitz, which was still in German hands, to get the latest news. Just before we took off again on the last stage of our journey, a telephoned order from Hitler arrived to the effect that in no circumstances was I to fly into Breslau. But here I could only follow my heart. I was still officially only a civilian employee of the Research Station at Darmstadt and was, therefore, not subject to military orders, even from Hitler himself. So I decided to disregard them and flew on, hedge-hopping the whole way to keep out of sight of Russian tanks. We arrived safely at Breslau, landing inside the besieged city. Here, as in Russia, I saw the full horror of war. While my companion went about his duties, I watched the pale, fear-ridden faces of the women and the old men, in whom speech had withered before the terrible fate that they knew awaited them.

In April, I was called to Breslau for the third time. I flew via Hirschberg, my home town, finding it almost emptied of civilians, but not yet occupied by the Russians. There a radio message reached me informing me that it was no longer necessary to fly on to Breslau.

Still in Hirschberg, I was ordered a few days later to report to Munich. Heavy in heart, I said goodbye to the Mayor, Oberbürgermeister Blasius, an old friend of my parents and a truly fine type of German. I knew that I would not see him or my beloved home again.

In Munich, I received orders to reconnoitre emergency landing grounds for hospital planes in the neighbourhood of Kitzbühl. But first, I had time to spend a whole day with my family in Salzburg, where my parents, my sister Heidi with her three children, and Anni, our faithful maid-of-all-work, were living as evacuees. Though overcast by the gathering clouds of the national tragedy, we were as happy as ever in our reunion.

On 25th April, in Kitzbühl, I received a message from Colonel-General von Greim ordering me to report at once to Munich for a special task. On the way there, I learnt that von Greim had been ordered by radio to report immediately to Adolf Hitler in the Reich Chancellery. As Berlin was now completely encircled and Russian troops were already in the city, von Greim had decided that the quickest way to reach the Reich Chancellery would be by helicopter. He remembered my training flights over the ruined city and knew that I would be able to find my bearings whatever the conditions. But, the military situation forcing him to assume that we would not return from the flight, he first asked my parents' permission for me to go. This they gave without hesitation.

It was midnight when I arrived in Salzburg to say goodbye to my parents. I found them waiting for me at the gateway to the house. They embraced me in silence. I went down into the air-raid shelter in the cellar to the sleeping children, took them up in turn and hugged them—and then, for the last time, looked in the eyes of my father and mother. Standing straight and motionless, they watched me as I climbed into my car and drove away.

The Ju 188, which was to fly us as far as Rechlin, took off at 2.30 a.m. from Neu-Bieberg, near Munich. Standing in the narrow fuselage, I looked out into the clear, star-lit night. Unexpectedly, there was no sign of the enemy planes which for weeks had dominated the German skies. The die was cast . . .

At 4 a.m. on 26th April, we landed at Rechlin. The Air Operations Staff (Northern Area) were stationed here and the news they gave us was very bad. For the past two days, not a single German plane had succeeded in penetrating the Russian defences and flying into Berlin. Of the Berlin airports only Gatow remained in German hands and it was now encircled and under continual artillery fire. It was not known whether there was still sufficient runway free of shell-craters on which to land. Finally, the helicopter which we had intended to land at night in front of the Reich Chancellery had just been destroyed in an air attack on Rechlin itself.

It was decided we should fly, instead, in a Focke Wulff 190, a single-seater fighter, as this was the fastest machine available at Rechlin. This particular plane had been fitted with a second seat in the luggage space and two days before had successfully flown Speer, the War Production Minister, into and out of Berlin. The pilot, a Luftwaffe Sergeant, held the record for flights into the beleaguered city and had an excellent knowledge of the Russian defence tactics and Ack-Ack positions.

He was therefore chosen to pilot von Greim, but, having landed him at Gatow, was to return immediately as the airport was expected hourly to be captured by the Russians. In that case, I wondered, how was von Greim to get from Gatow, on the outskirts ,to the Reich Chancellery, which lay in the very heart of the city? The flight from the perimeter to the centre of Berlin would certainly be the hardest part of the journey, but thanks to my training flights to the Ack-Ack tower, the course was known to me in every detail and I therefore made up my mind that I would go with them to Gatow.

I went on to the airfield where I found the pilot preparing for the flight. I asked him if it would add to his difficulties if he took me with him. He laughed: "Your weight wouldn't matter much, but there's no room." That remained to be seen. There might possibly be room for me in the rear of the fuselage, though it was crammed with accumulators, oxygen cylinders and other gear.

With a good deal of assistance, I was literally threaded, feet first, through a space in the rear section of the fuselage, where I lay in total darkness wedged in on top of the sharp metal frame-members. Once there, I found I could not move an inch and knew I would never be able to get out again unaided.

The most terrifying pictures began to chase through my mind and suddenly I found myself possessed by a terror such as I had never before experienced. But I could not give in now—somehow it had to be mastered.

Meanwhile, the airfield had come to life. Thirty or forty fighters which had been detailed to escort us were shaking the air with their roar. I could not remember when I had last seen so large a concentration of German planes together and the mere thought of their presence gave me strength.

Soon after, General von Greim arrived and took his seat in the plane. I made no sound until we were signalled to take off, then I called to him from my hide-out. For a moment there came no answer, then I heard his voice, loud and searching: "Kapitän, where are you?"

I had just time to tell him before we began to bump over the rough runway and the metal spars made themselves painfully felt.

If all went well, we should reach Gatow in about thirty minutes, but the "if" was a big one. The air over Berlin was patrolled incessantly by enemy fighters and they would be sure to drop on us like hawks.

Surprisingly, the flight was uneventful until we were just short of Berlin. But each minute that I counted on the luminous dial of my watch seemed like a separate eternity. Never before had I flown in such an agony of suspense, so completely helpless a prey to any grim, unforeseen fate that might await us.

Suddenly—we must by now have reached the area of Greater Berlin—the plane pitched on to its nose and with screaming exhausts plummeted vertically earthwards.

Even greater than the physical strain—I was rocketing down head-first—was the suspense, for the only possible explanation seemed to be that the plane had been hit and in a matter of seconds it would surely strike the ground and go up in flames. I had no idea that the pilot was diving to avoid some attacking Russian fighters; I only felt how, after a while, he steadied the machine and lifted her nose. Shortly after we touched down at Gatow Airport.

As soon as we touched the earth, we made a dash for the Control Officer's air-raid shelter. Greim set about trying to contact the Reich Chancellery by telephone and with the greatest difficulty finally got through, though with continual interruptions. In reply to Greim's question, Colonel von Below, Hitler's Luftwaffe Adjutant, said that Hitler wished to speak to him at all costs, but had not stated the reason. Von Below said that all approach roads into the city were now in Russian hands and, in the inner city itself, the Anhalter Station and parts of the Bülowstrasse and the Potsdamerstrasse.

Though it now seemed well nigh impossible to reach the Chancellery, Greim felt it was his duty to obey orders whatever the cost, and so, after careful thought, we finally decided to try and fly into Berlin in a Fieseler Storch and land by the Brandenburg Gate.

Just before we were due to start, the plane we were to use was destroyed by artillery fire. It was almost 6 p.m. before the only remaining "Storch" could take off and, as I had no experience of flying under fire, Greim insisted on piloting it himself. As a precaution, I tested before we left the ground whether, standing behind the pilot's seat, I should be able to reach the stick and throttle over his left shoulder.

The plane lifted smoothly from the ground, Greim keeping her as low as he possibly could. Beneath us, the waters of the Wannsee gleamed silver in the failing light—remote, idyllic peace. But the scene only flickered across my consciousness, riveted with animal concentration on the surrounding danger. We reached the Grunewald without interference, almost brushing the tree-tops to avoid the enemy fighters now appearing everywhere above us. Suddenly, from the ground, out of the shadows, from the tree-tops themselves, leapt the very fires of Hell, concentrating from every quarter on us, seemingly us alone. Below, Russian tanks and soldiers were swarming among the trees. I could see clearly the men's faces, as rifles, tommy-guns and anti-tank weapons were raised and fired at us. We were haloed and flanked and underlined with innumerable and deadly little explosive puffs.

Then, suddenly, there was a rending crash—I saw a yellowy-white flame streak up beside the engine and, at the same time, Greim shouted that he was hit—an armour-piercing bullet had smashed through his right foot. Mechanically, I stretched over his shoulder, seized throttle and stick and struggled to keep the machine twisting and turning to avoid the fire. Greim lay crumpled in his seat, unconscious. The air was exploding continually around us, the din drowning our own engine. Again and again we were hit. With a spasm of terror, I caught sight of petrol running from both wing-tanks. An explosion, I thought, was inevitable, should have happened already. And still the plane answered the controls and still I remained untouched. But I was very anxious about Greim. Several times he started up, his hand grasped with convulsive energy for the stick and then fell away as once more he lost consciousness.

We were now approaching the Radio Tower and the evil-smelling, sulphurous air whirled thicker and thicker with smoke, dust and fumes. Visibility was almost nil. The ground-fire was slackening and the area seemed, at any rate, to be still in German hands. It was here that my training flights over Berlin proved their use. To have flown around searching for landmarks would have been asking for trouble, but fortunately this was unnecessary, as I remembered the compass-bearing of the Ack-Ack tower. This lay directly on our route and I now headed towards it. From there I could not fail to find the broad highway running straight East and West through Berlin. At the eastern end of it lay the Branden-burg Gate and when I finally landed just short of it, there was hardly a drop of petrol left in the tank.

Von Greim had meanwhile regained consciousness and, with great difficulty, I helped him out of the machine, which might at any moment be spotted and attacked. He sat down at the side of the road. Now we could only wait and wait, on the off-chance that some vehicle might come our way—we could only hope it would not be a Russian one.

The whole area around the Brandenburg Gate seemed deserted, lifeless, extinct. A silent horror seeped from the jagged and gaping pillboxes that lay all around. The minutes dragged on funereally. Once, somewhere close at hand, came several sharp cracks—then a soundless desolation reigned once more.

I cannot remember how long we had waited when at last we sighted a German lorry. We climbed in and were driven through the Brandenburg Gate, along Unter den Linden, through the Wilhelmstrasse and into the Vossstrasse. I could not reconcile the devastation of rubble and charred wreckage, the all-pervading blanket of smoke, with the proud, imposing buildings that once lined these streets. It was as if a drop-screen had been lowered, hiding the familiar reality.

We drew up at the entrance to the air-raid Bunker of the Reich Chancellery. SS Guards carried the General to the underground operating theatre, where Hitler's surgeon, Dr. Stumpfecker, at once took charge of him. After his wound had been treated, the General, lying on a stretcher, and I were conducted two floors lower down to the Führerbunker. As we arrived, Frau Goebbels was coming out of the entrance. I had never seen her before but recognized her from photographs. For a moment she stared at us in wide-eyed amazement, as if in wonder that anything living should have found its way there. Then, sobbing, she clasped me in her arms.

In the narrow passage-hall of the Führerbunker we met Adolf Hitler. His head drooped heavily on his shoulders and a continual twitching affected both his arms. The eyes were glassy and remote. He greeted us in an expressionless voice.

Greim reported on our journey, Hitler listening calmly and attentively. When he had finished, Hitler seized both Greim's hands and then, turning to me: "Brave woman! So there is still some loyalty and courage left in the world!"

Hitler told Greim why he had summoned him. He believed that Göring had betrayed him. He produced the telegram, since become famous, in which Göring had asked to be confirmed as Hitler's successor.

"Nothing is spared me," shouted Hitler, "nothing! Every disillusion, every betrayal, dishonour, treason has been heaped upon me. I have had Göring put under immediate arrest, stripped him of all his offices, expelled him from all Party Organisations."

Then Hitler appointed Greim as Chief of the Luftwaffe, in place of Göring, with promotion to the rank of Field-Marshal, to take effect forthwith.

There was silence. I glanced at the face of the new Field-Marshal who stood there tight-lipped and motionless. It was not difficult to guess what thoughts and feelings this appointment had aroused in him. Commander-in-Chief of an Air Force that no longer existed! In the circumstances and for him, whose conception of honour was entirely immutable and selfless, it could have only one meaning—to stay here, in the Bunker, with Hitler, to the end. And if Greim stayed, then I would stay with him.

The circle in which we found ourselves was small. On the lowest floor of the Bunker lived Hitler, Eva Braun, Goebbels and Hitler's surgeon, Dr. Stumpfecker. On the floor above were accommodated the following:

Martin Bormann, Head of the Party Secretariat and Hitler's "Personal Secretary."

State-Secretary Naumann, Goebbels' Assistant in the Propaganda Ministry.

Ambassador Hevel, Representative of Ribbentrop at Hitler's H.Q.

Admiral Voss, Naval Liaison Officer.

Colonel von Below, Hitler's Luftwaffe Adjutant.

General Krebs, Chief of the Army General Staff.

General Burgdorf, Hitler's Army Adjutant.

Baur, Betz, Hitler's Pilots.

Frau Christian, Frau Jung, Hitler's Secretaries.

Frl. Krüger, Bormann's Secretary.

Heinz Lorenz, Official of the German News Agency.

Rattenhuber, Head of Detective Force responsible for Hitler's personal safety.

Fegelein, Representative of Himmler at Hitler's H.Q.

All these I knew by sight, but that was all.

Frau Goebbels had voluntarily chosen to remain with her children in the Bunker rather than leave Berlin and shortly after our first conversation with Hitler, she took me to her room on the top floor to have a much-needed wash. Thereafter, when I was not nursing von Greim, I devoted myself to her children, aged between four and twelve.

As I entered her room that first evening, I was confronted with six little faces peering at me with lively curiosity from their double-decker bunks. To meet someone who could fly opened wide for them the door of their childhood imagination and while I was washing, my nerves still on edge from the strain of the last few hours, they bombarded me with questions, jostling me willy-nilly into their own lively little world. After that, they summoned me at each meal-time to tell them about the strange lands and peoples that I had seen, or to describe my flights or to recount their favourite fairy stories. Each one of them was a delight with its open-hearted naturalness and bright intelligence.

Their concern for each other was touching. One little girl was isolated for a time in the next room with tonsilitis and when telling a story to the others, I had to pause every so often, so that one of them could tell the patient next door "what happened next." I taught them part-songs and how to yodel in real Tyrolean style. The crash and thunder of the shells bursting above failed to disturb them. It was their "Uncle Führer," as they had been told, busy conquering his enemies, and when the youngest got frightened and began to cry, he was quickly pacified with this explanation.

As the tension mounted hour by hour and finally became almost unbearable, while the whole world around us was crumbling, this little oasis of happiness and peace remained unaltered. The contrast caused me more suffering than anything else; sometimes I felt I could stand no more. Before the children went to sleep, I used to sing with them, "To-morrow

and it be His Will, the Lord shall wake thee once again."
To-morrow . . .?

The remaining occupants of the Bunker bore themselves
with calmness and resolution, but I only met them occasionally and by chance.

The very first night that I spent in the Bunker (26th
April) was one of continuous alarm and no one thought of
sleep. The Russians had at last got the range of the Reich
Chancellery. The artillery fire above us continued without
pause and with increasing fury. Even in the lower floor, fifty
feet below ground, mortar rained from the walls.

All of us knew without shadow of doubt that the end was
coming hourly nearer and the knowledge seemed to paralyse
thought and will. In spite of, or perhaps because of, this
certainty, hope could not altogether be suppressed. Those in
Hitler's immediate circle were completely cut off from the
outside world, where a desperate battle raged for what
remained of Berlin and Germany and, misled by rumours
and scraps of news, they were repeatedly uttering fresh
hopes of rescue, even hopes that Berlin would be relieved.
To those who, like ourselves, had only recently reached the
Bunker, their self-deception was particularly noticeable.

Although the occupants of the Bunker were confined in
the smallest space and would share the same fate, perhaps
in a matter of hours, von Greim and I, because we had just
arrived from the outside world, felt ourselves separate from
the others, as if we were onlookers. This sense of distance
increased as the tension mounted.

To us, it was clear that Hitler and his immediate circle
were living in a world of their own, far removed from the
reality outside, where a desperate battle raged for what
remained of Berlin and Germany. Hopes of rescue, nourished
by rumour and occasional items of favourable news, led them
to adopt a fantastically distorted picture of the truth.

The next two days (27th and 28th April) brought no
developments fundamentally altering the situation. We lived
hour by hour on a rack of suspense, now and then screwed
yet higher by a new hope born of illusion or by some news of

fresh disaster, which spread among us with lightning speed. It was rumoured that Fegelein, the brother-in-law of Eva Braun, for many years liaison officer between Himmler and Hitler, had been accused of attempted desertion and shot on Hitler's orders. This piece of news made me feel that the very ground beneath my feet was beginning to give way.

The announcement that a Ju 52 had landed on the East-West Axis to fetch Greim and me out of Berlin sounded, on the other hand, like a miracle. But Greim refused to go, repeating his refusal over the telephone to Rudel, who had got through on the last remaining line from Rechlin to tell him that the plane was on its way.

Meanwhile, as the Russians steadily advanced the weight of the attack on the Reich Chancellery increased hour by hour and we gave up all hope of seeing daylight again.

On our second day in the Bunker, 27th April, I was summoned to Hitler's study. His face was now even paler, and had become flaccid and putty-coloured, like that of a dotard. He gave me two phials of poison so that, as he said, Greim and I should have at all times "freedom of choice." Then he said that if the hope of the relief of Berlin by General Wenk was not realized, he and Eva Braun had freely decided that they would depart out of this life.

My impression was that, even if the hopes which Hitler pinned on Wenk's Army were realized, his vital energies were by now too depleted to sustain him alive. But events would surely follow a different course. He had just been presented with opportunities of escape, but had rejected them as out of the question, once when a Ju 52 landed on the East-West Axis and again, when an Arado 96 got through. He believed that his presence in Berlin would make a decisive difference to the defenders' morale: indeed, this thought alone was keeping him alive.

And now came the night of 28th April. One after another, tornadoes of fire swept down on the Reich Chancellery. It was rumoured that the Russians had reached the entrance to the Wilhelmstrasse and had advanced as far as the Potsdamer Platz.

Shortly after midnight, Hitler suddenly appeared in the doorway to Greim's sick-room, his face ashen-white, like a dead man's. He was clutching a wireless message and a map. "Now Himmler has betrayed me . . . You two must leave the Bunker as quickly as you can. I have had news that the Russians are going to storm the Reich Chancellery to-morrow morning." He opened the map. "If the enemy con-centrations in the streets leading to the Reich Chancellery can be destroyed by air attack, we can gain at least twenty-four hours and enable General Wenk to reach us in time . . . Already at Potsdam they can hear his artillery fire." Then, he told us that an Arado 96 had succeeded in landing on the East-West Axis and was at our disposal.

I had no knowledge of military matters, but it seemed to me incredible that at this stage any idea of a relief could be entertained. I thought of the scenes that in the last few weeks had met our eyes in every part of Germany, of the roads and tracks blocked and overflowing with fleeing civilians, the troops flooding back from the front, the nights spent amid the moan and crash of bombs, the bombardment under which the Reich Chancellery had lain for days—surely no General Wenk could reverse this tide?

But the world of illusion still stubbornly persisted. As Greim and I were making ready to leave, Frau Goebbels beseeched us in tears to do everything possible to bring about the relief of the Bunker. Then, regaining the wonderful com-posure that had never left her since our first meeting, she gave me a letter for her son by her first marriage. Her chil-dren were asleep: I did not see them again.

Hitler was in the Map Room and bade me farewell with a cursory handshake and a muttered "God protect you!" I could find nothing appropriate to say. From the others also we parted without a word.

Colonel von Below accompanied us—von Greim painfully hobbling on crutches—as far as the exit of the Bunker. The sulphurous, smoke-laden air became thicker as we approached the surface and when we stopped out into the Vossstrasse, the sky was a billowing sea of smoke and yellowy-red flame, while our ears drummed ceaselessly with the wail and crash of shells.

In a lull in the firing, we requisitioned an armoured car and began an eerie journey through the ruined street. We had to take a chance on whether we encountered the Russians en route and we breathed a sigh of relief when we had safely passed the corner of the Vossstrasse and the Hermann Göringstrasse. We drove through the Tiergarten to the Victory Column, which was still in German hands. The aircraft was standing in a blast-bay. To have landed here, with the East-West Axis under continual fire, was an amazing feat. It turned out to be the same pilot who had flown us to Gatow.

Dispatch-riders reported that the Axis was clear of shell-craters for four hundred yards, but that the situation might alter at any moment.

Though enemy searchlights were groping continually up and down the Axis, we managed to take off without being spotted and headed towards the Brandenburg Gate. Flying past, I caught a glimpse of it silhouetted in the glare of searchlights. We flew on, undisturbed by spasmodic tracer fire, and in about a mile reached the welcoming protection of a cloud-bank. When we emerged, the sky was moon-lit and clear. Heading in the direction of Rechlin, we passed over the province of Brandenburg, the blackness threaded with silver-gleaming lakes and punctuated with the red dots of the burning villages that everywhere marked the route of war and destruction.

We landed at Rechlin at about three in the morning, being welcomed in silence by what remained of the Operations Staff. Shivering, weary and oppressed, I stamped about to get warm, breathing in the cold, night air. It seemed that even here I could already smell fire, doom and death ...

After Field-Marshal von Greim had held a conference with the staff at Rechlin, we flew to Plön to Grand-Admiral Dönitz and soon after to Dobbin, to see Field-Marshal Keitel. The small "Bücker" plane which I had chosen to fly

was easy to handle and had a good field of vision. I avoided
roads and railway lines, as these were a continual target for
low-flying attacks and instead, crept rather than flew as low
as I could along the fringe of woods, almost brushing the
hedges and fences as I passed over them. Some stretches of
the journey had to be covered by road, but motoring turned
out to be no less dangerous than flying. Time and again we
had to stop, while I helped the wounded von Greim to take
cover at the roadside. It was at Lübeck, during the night of
30th April, that we heard the radio announcement of Hitler's
death and the formation of the new German Government
under Dönitz.

Greim was impatient to get to his command in Bohemia
and after another short visit to Plön to see Dönitz, we flew in
a Dornier 217 to Königgrätz. Greim was already suffering
from a severe attack of nettlerash, contracted as the result of
an anti-tetanus injection. For four days he lay in hospital in
Königgrätz while events in Germany were moving swiftly.
On May 7th, still in hospital, news reached him that the
Capitulation would probably be signed on the 9th.

Before deciding what orders to issue to the Luftwaffe,
Greim wanted to contact General Field-Marshal Kesselring.
The latter was said to be at Zell-am-See and thither we flew,
in two machines, via Graz. After a wonderfully peaceful
flight over the Alps, we landed at Zell-am-See, only to hear
that Germany had signed an unconditional surrender.
Greim's command was already at an end.

Still needing treatment, Greim was admitted to the civilian
hospital in Kitzbühl and it was in Kitzbühl, with the entry
of the American troops into the town, that we saw the final
collapse of all our hopes.

## 29. I Live to Fly Again

AMID THE chaos of defeat, I found consolation and
security in the knowledge that my family were close by,
living as refugees in Salzburg. I was anxious to send news to
them and at last I found someone who would take them a
message. But they no longer answered. Only seven mounds
of earth remained as tokens of those who had been nearest
to me in this world.

In the days preceding the entry of the Americans, a
rumour had spread that all refugees were to be taken back to
their original homes. My father knew what that would mean
for the women and children who had lived in the Eastern
territories, for he had been called to work there as a doctor
in some of the temporarily reoccupied villages. Feeling an
overriding duty to preserve his own family from being
surrendered to the Russians, ignorant of my own fate and
believing my brother to have been killed, he had seen no
alternative but to take upon himself the heaviest responsibility
of all.

As for me, I tried to live on—as a prisoner of the Americans, enduring all the crass vicissitudes of a "High Criminal
Person."

My offence? I was a German, well known as an airwoman
and as one who cherished an ardent love of her country and
had done her duty to the last. Legends formed about my last
flight into Berlin. Might I not perhaps have hidden Hitler
away somewhere?

First, I was taken from Kitzbühl to a villa in Gmund,
where they treated me with courteous consideration. Perhaps
I could be persuaded to reveal the secret? After that, I was
hustled, with blows from American rifle-butts, into a prison
cell. Here I learnt the degradation of captivity, living
between narrow walls through a monotony of days, gazing

longingly to where, high above my head, a patch of sky could be glimpsed through the bars of a tiny window.

Then I was loaded on to a jeep and taken on a nine-hour journey, at a furious speed and over atrocious roads, to an internment camp. There I was put into a cell about the size of a railway sleeping compartment, completely bare except for a straw mattress on the floor, with one barred window, denuded of glass, through which the cold October air streamed in unhindered.

Was that the America that I had known and loved? I could not think so, for the face I saw was hardened in hate.

Some time later, after I had been moved to the Alaska Internee Camp in Oberursel, an American General came to see me, and he was different—frank, open-hearted and kind, like the Americans I remembered. Later I got to know his wife, a grey-haired woman with beautiful, clear features—she, too, had the victor's mentality of 1945.

Through my own experience in Germany, I had seen how official propaganda had not only perverted the truth, but blinded the people to a sense of their own guilt. Talking with the General and his wife, I now realised that this applied no less to the victors. Neither of them was petty-minded or vindictive, like the Americans who guarded and interrogated me, but I could see that even they had been affected by anti-German propaganda, sincere and generous as they were. So perhaps it was not American brutality that was responsible for my sufferings as a prisoner, but the self-inflicted blindness of nations at war.

After a time, I was moved to an internment camp in Oberursel and from there, in October 1946 after fifteen months' captivity, I was finally released.

And now, free once more, I can see, from the open windows of the house where I am living, the delicate cloud-veils as they form in the clear blue Summer sky. They slowly gather shape, then as slowly disperse and fade away.

I am longing to fly again!

I long to be soaring up into those timeless and hallowed

spaces, whose beauty compels all true airmen to be a belief
in God.

I am longing to fly again—into the clouds, the wind and
the sky. There I would love to be sailing now in my glider,
silently, the earth far below. With my hand on the control-
column, my eyes look skywards, over the shimmering wings.
I am filled with awe, for about me all is silence.

The glider is sailing down now, carrying me back to earth.
It comes nearer and nearer. The mountains rear up, the hills
fall away into plain, towns rise before my eyes.

In itself, the earth is the same—but in me, it has changed.

He who has drawn nigh to God must also be close to Man.

That is the truth which flying has taught me. Human
inventiveness, learning, technical science can achieve nothing, if heart and soul do *not* keep pace with the development.
They are the conscience which compels respect for the Divine
Order. Have we not long since lost the human being in our
neighbour? We will only find him again when we have
regained our piety.

And it is the task of all us airmen to bring back with us to
earth what we have experienced in the sky. There can be no
better instrument for peace and reconciliation than our
beloved gliding.

Flying—that is my life. Flight over the earth is its symbol.
May flying in future serve only to bring men and peoples
closer together.

## Postscript to The Sky my Kingdom by Hanna Reitsch

I wrote this book after I had been released from one and a half years as a prisoner of war in the United States. Its purpose was not just to deal with my own life as a pilot, but also to show what many German people thought in and about the past and about what it was we stood for. My life since then has been very varied in its ups and downs, and in its meetings with unusual people, heads of state, astronauts, and people from many countries, continents and races. Quite apart from all this, I have been lucky enough to achieve much greater success in the field of sporting aviation than was the case before 1945.

I found this book comparatively easy to write since I only had to tell the truth and to set it down frankly. Since then I have discovered that telling the truth can be wounding. The most difficult thing for me to bear has been the way my flight with Generaloberst Ritter von Greim (the last commander-in-chief of the former Luftwaffe) to Berlin, then completely encircled by the Russians, was so misrepresented. The slurs continue to this day whenever my name appears in a newspaper. I was, and still am, again and again put into a political arena where I have never belonged. Even today, so-called eye-witness reports about the last days in Hitler's Bunker appear under my name in the German and international press and in books. They contain or use notes that the American Counter-Intelligence Corps published in December 1945. I wish to state categorically that I never wrote these accounts (which appear within quotation marks); I have never seen them and I have never signed them. They do not, in most respects, represent what really happened. My encounters with leading personalities came about because of my work. I write about them, as about the rest of my life: where I come from, how I came to take up my profession, and what I was lucky enough to experience as a pilot up to 1945.

In contrast to my account of that last flight to Berlin with Generaloberst Ritter von Greim, these so-called eye-witness reports ignore the fact that I had been picked for this mission because I was a pilot and a trusted friend, and instead call me "Hitler's girl-friend". I can only assume that the inventor of these incorrect accounts did not realise what the consequences would be for my life. Ever since then I have been accused of many things in connection with the Third Reich, both at home and abroad, and particularly in the Eastern countries. Yet in spite of everything, I have been lucky enough to achieve great success in flying since 1952 when we Germans were allowed to fly again: I was the first woman glider pilot to compete in the 1952 world championship in Madrid where I won the German Aero-Club bronze medal for Germany. It was on that occasion that a French Jew, who had lost a leg and an arm in the battle against Germany, approached me. He took my hand and said: "You have won the hearts of everyone in these world championships." This to me was more moving than the event itself.

In 1955 there was a high point in my career when, again as the only woman competitor, I won the German championship, although the then gliding world champion, the Frenchman Pierre and the former champion the Swede Silsmo took part as guest flyers. I then took part successfully in the 1956 world gliding championship at St Yan in France, where I achieved a new German women's record in free long-distance gliding of 370 km. A particular success came in France in 1957 with a height of 6,848 m over St Auban in a wave of aircraft. This was a new German women's glider record and I won the first diamond of the 'Gold C.

Something happened in 1958 which meant I would never fly again in Germany. I was invited by the German Aero-Club to participate in a world gliding championship in Poland, and I was the only pilot who was refused an entrance visa. As the German national team went on to participate without protest, I decided not to fly in any further events with this club.

A year later, however, I took up an invitation to India to assist gliding there. This experience with its insight into that vast continent and its impressions of India's spiritual life and particularly the friendship I formed with the wise Indian

Prime Minister Jawaharlal Nehru, with whom I flew high over New Delhi in a glider, was to become of great importance in my future life. Through Pandit Nehru in whose house I stayed I received a fascinating introduction to yoga with daily exercises and meditation. But I did not know then what a fateful path Pandit Nehru would cause me to follow.

In 1961 I accepted an invitation from American gliding pilots to take part in a flight by a wave of aircraft over the Sierra Nevada. The voyage was enriched by some highly interesting events: a visit to the famous US research station Edwards Air Force Base in California; an invitation to Huntsville, Alabama to see Wernher von Braun, a reception at the White House given by President Kennedy, and an encounter with the great scientist and constructor Igor Sikorsky in Connecticut.

In the autumn of that year the Finnish Aeroclub invited me to Finland, a country that I have been close to since 1934. Then, however, a new world opened up for me: Black Africa. Pandit Nehru had, in January 1962, suggested to his friend Dr Kwame Nkrumah, the president of Ghana, that he should aske me to open a gliding school in his country which was to assist character forming for the youth of Ghana.

The coup staged in Ghana during the time of Dr Nkrumah's absence on a visit to Hanoi to discuss an end to the Vietnam war, put a sudden end to this – the most beautiful task of my life. I was arrested and deported.

And since? After that I took up flying helicopters again – in 1937 I was the first woman ever to do this – and undertook systematic gliding flights over the Alps. 1937 had also been the year that I made my first crossing of the Alps in a glider from Salzburg to Italy. I found that gliding over the Alps from 1969 onwards brought me many spiritual rewards. I have continued to meet many interesting people, scientists, sportsmen and test-pilots – including Neil Armstrong, the first man on the moon.

We flying people of the world have an important task: to carry back to earth what we experience high above. Up there, there are no frontiers, no nations, no languages – up there, everything is part of a unity. The loneliness of flight in this vast emptiness has made our souls brothers.

May flying people help the cause of world peace!

Hanna Reitsch

*This postscript has been taken from a new edition of* THE SKY MY KINGDOM *published in Germany before Hanna Reitsch's death in 1979.*

A full and objective account of the life of Hanna Reitsch, including interviews with her wartime colleagues and post-war interrogators, has been written by Judy Lomax: *Hanna Reitsch: Flying for the Fatherland* (John Murray).

# Index

223